100 Ideas for Primary Teachers:

Interventions

Stephen Lockyer

B L O O M S B U R Y

LONDON • OXFORD • NEW YORK • NEW DELHI • SYDNEY

BLOOMSBURY EDUCATION
Bloomsbury Publishing Plc
50 Bedford Square, London, WC1B 3DP, UK

BLOOMSBURY, BLOOMSBURY EDUCATION and
the Diana logo are trademarks of Bloomsbury Publishing Plc

First published in Great Britain, 2018

A catalogue record for this book is available from the British Library.

ISBN: PB: 978-1-4729-4966-0; ePDF: 978-1-4729-4965-3;
ePub: 978-1-4729-4963-9

2 4 6 8 10 9 7 5 3

Typeset by Newgen KnowledgeWorks Pvt. Ltd., Chennai, India
Printed and bound by CPI Group (UK) Ltd, Croydon CR0 4YY

All papers used by Bloomsbury Publishing Plc are natural, recyclable products
from wood grown in well-managed forests. The manufacturing processes
conform to the environmental regulations of the country of origin.

To find out more about our authors and books visit
www.bloomsbury.com and sign up for our newsletters.

Contents

Acknowledgements

Many thanks to my merry band of supporters for their help, guidance and ideas, some of which are contained within this book. I wrote this book because there was no book out there with ideas I could grab and use, as quickly as I needed, to correct the direction and aspiration of the children within my care. Thanks also to the lovely Bloomsbury team, past and present, for your support and tolerance of me. Lastly, thanks to all those teachers who let me use their ideas in this book, as well as both Shirley and Kelly – two of the finest and most outstanding teaching assistants I have worked with in the past ten(ish) years. May your classrooms never be sullied by my singing or my impromptu ideas.

Introduction

Every day, in almost every primary classroom across the UK, children are extracted from main lessons to top up their knowledge and plug gaps that have appeared or grown. These interventions are essential for getting children who have fallen behind back in line with their peers, but are often hurried, snatched moments of microteaching, carried out with less planning than the main lesson.

To top it all, these sessions can be led by teaching assistants, the unsung heroes of modern teaching. The complexities and challenges of primary teaching often leave little space for teachers to plan or even track interventions. As a result, a lot of the thinking work, and sometimes even the ideas, is left up to teaching assistants, who may also be busy preparing for break duty, whilst simultaneously sorting the book bag pile.

This book is filled to the brim with ideas for these sessions. Some ideas are tailored for individuals, while others are perfect for group work. They use a minimum of resources, except where essential, and any purchases cost a maximum of five pounds (but can often be found around school somewhere). There are sections on planning and making an intervention work, utilising the time and space most effectively, and lots of ideas on everyday top-up areas we seek to resolve with these children, including spelling, reading, number correspondence and handwriting.

If you have the time, write down every child you think needs an intervention and their number-one need, then find the most appropriate section in the book. Put a sticky note in that section and hand it to whoever is going to lead the intervention for you. If you really don't have the time, pass this book to them with an earnest, pleading look and enjoy the results.

How to use this book

This book includes quick, easy and practical ideas for you to dip in and out of, to support you in planning and conducting effective interventions.

Each idea includes:

- a catchy title, easy to refer to and share with your colleagues
- an interesting quote linked to the idea
- a summary of the idea in bold, making it easy to flick through the book and identify an idea you want to use at a glance
- a step-by-step guide to implementing the idea.

Each idea also includes one or more of the following:

Teaching tip

Practical tips and advice for how and how not to run the activity or put the idea into practice.

Taking it further

Ideas and advice for how to extend the idea or develop it further.

Bonus idea ★

There are six bonus ideas in this book that are extra exciting, extra original and extra interesting.

#hashtags
To prompt further exploration and discussion of the idea online.

Share how you use these ideas and find out what other practitioners have done using **#100ideas**.

Tips for effective interventions

Part 1

Planning an intervention

'I know now how to make the best use of my time.'

Sometimes, you can be asked to carry out an intervention to solve a particular problem, but don't know exactly what to do or even how to start! Follow these tips for planning a successful intervention.

Start with the end in mind

Establish in your head exactly what you want the end point of the intervention to look like. Detail this as much as possible, as you will need to ensure you are feeding all of these particular fires. If it is to encourage enthusiasm for reading, for example, this must be a key component of your intervention.

Find the baseline

You need to understand the level at which the child is currently working in order to know where to go. You can gather anecdotal evidence at first, but try to formalise this in some way. Often, this can be as simple as photocopying some work they have produced.

Solo or small group

Depending on the task, you need to decide whether the intervention is best carried out as a solo activity or as part of a small group. It is best not to let a group exceed four in number. Choose the group dynamic based on your involvement as the adult. If you will be called on for support near constantly, opt for solo work with one child. Be aware that for some tasks, groups working together create a strong dynamic.

Cut the fluff

You want the children working 100% of the time in interventions. Make the sessions active and pacy. Plunge straight in with little to no teacher talk at the start. Boredom is the killer of interventions – interventions should be seen as an absolute, indulgent treat for the child.

Rehearse the activity beforehand

This is when partners or your own children can help out – design your intervention and carry out the intervention with your guinea pigs. Try where possible not to use anyone who works in education as they will hold a different viewpoint than someone cold to the task. The aim here is to ensure your instructions are crystal clear and you have all the equipment necessary.

Taking it further

Treat the ideas in this book as a launch pad for other ideas. Please do share any variations on the activities outlined online using the hashtag alongside each idea and let @mrlockyer and @BloomsburyEd know.

#planning

Observe an intervention

'I can see where I was wasting time and the children were getting bored.'

Observation is the key to improving your interventions. Here are the best three ways of doing this.

Observe someone else

Speak to your inclusion manager about your desire to observe someone who is really good at interventions. This should take little time to organise and happen. Make sure you note down everything you observe. It was observing a brilliant teaching assistant once that made me realise that a good intervention is like cooking in a caravan – everything is on hand and you shouldn't have to move. Thank them afterwards, telling them what you noticed, and take this to your own practice.

Have someone observe you

Deep breath – this is not as onerous as you might imagine! You will improve no end by getting positive feedback as well as constructive guidance on how to improve. Have them monitor levels of engagement, what children do when they are off-task, use of resources and use of voice. They really must be brutally honest. Remember, this isn't a formal observation or performance management – this is upskilling. I have never NOT learnt something about my own practice by being observed.

Film yourself

Perhaps the least threatening option. Set up a tablet to record yourself and film the whole thing. This is both fascinating and insightful, and was where I identified how many questions I asked of pupils that I then answered myself.

#observation

Intervention journeys

'I love my intervention group from start to finish.'

How many minutes a week do you spend waiting for children? Utilise this dead time by building the journey time into the intervention. Stop sending for children and start collecting them!

If your intervention space is quite a distance from your classroom, make the journey a feature. As you collect the child, engage in conversation with them. This helps you to identify how they are feeling today, if there are any worries that might affect the intervention itself, and even if they have been practising their words or sums at home with their adults.

Likewise, on the journey back (to collect the next child), test them on things they have covered in the intervention. If you meet an adult en route, have a chat about just how well the child has been working and get them to tell the other adult what they have been doing. This gives the intervention a status it often lacks.

This takes no extra time than you would spend waiting for the child to arrive or return to class, but adds so much to the total experience.

Teaching tip

If you don't think that time is wasted, time everything one morning and add up all the minutes you spend waiting for children if you use the 'errand' method of collecting and returning children to class. You will surprise yourself.

#journeys

5

Star work

'I am really careful about which work I put my star on.'

One difficulty about interventions is that they often happen outside the classroom and thus away from the eyes of the teacher. This little strategy addresses this imbalance and also helps the child in question to view their work through a different lens.

Buy a selection of neon card stars or equivalent from a high street discount shop. Give three to each of the intervention children and explain that they have just three for the entire year. Explain that they get to award their work a star if they are especially proud of it. This starred work will then be shown to their teacher and, if they are comfortable, to the rest of their class.

This develops a dialogue between the child and the intervention leader at the end of any piece of work. You can discuss whether the work is of 'star standard' and if not, why not. It encourages the child to look critically at their work without being disparaging about their achievements.

You might find three stars too limiting and may wish to make it a 'three stars each half term' system. Alternatively, you could paper-clip the stars to the work so these can be moved to another, better, piece of work in the future.

#starwork

Back at basecamp

'I am working really well in class now.'

The aim of any intervention is to improve the life chances of the child you are with, not that they do well in the intervention. Any good intervention will be drawn upon in class too, as frequently as possible.

We all know the pressure teachers are under in terms of managing a team of children, then adults are added into that mix. If you have been given an intervention to lead, make it your own. Report regularly to the class teacher on what you are doing and the achievements made during this time (email is perfect for this, and can often simply be a one-liner at the end of the week).

Even more importantly, put back into the classroom what the child has worked on in their intervention. Highlight the links to them as they happen and use the tools you use out of class in the class too – otherwise you are effectively setting the child up for a fall. Utilise these opportunities to share with the rest of the children on that table the exact things you have been working on and the little tactics they can use too – they will be grateful.

Where possible, explicitly praise the use of intervention strategies in your marking. This can take seconds to do, yet is valuable not only for the teacher, but as a prompt for the child too.

Teaching tip

Communicate successful interventions with the rest of the teaching team – it is rare that a problem is unique to one child, and in any case, a good intervention can be adapted to suit a particular child's needs.

Taking it further

Set up a shared document within school and note down all the interventions as a central resource for all adults to contribute to and draw from.

#backinclass

7

Build your baseline

'I can demonstrate impact with ease.'

This sounds painfully obvious, but ensure you have a baseline for any intervention you lead. This may even be the first piece of work where you noticed that the child has some difficulty.

If there is ever any doubt as to the benefit of your interventions, you want to have evidence at the ready. It is no longer enough to simply say, 'but look at the difference in their reading/writing/maths now!'

To evidence your interventions, answer these three quite brutal questions:

1. So what?
2. What is the impact?
3. How do you know?

Of course, the best way of having evidence is to record changes as they occur, but providing a baseline and a current picture is inordinately helpful. If you have doubts as to the accuracy of the child's reading, carry out a running record at the start, and at regular intervals throughout. This is a great way of getting an insight into what gaps you need to plug straight away too.

Keep your records as clear as possible. One way of doing this is to imagine that you are sick one day and someone has to take over your intervention. In an ideal world, they should be able to pick up your folder and see exactly where the child is, and what you do with them.

#baselinecheck

Winning ladders

'This makes me realise how much I can do.'

Interventions can flash past without anyone seeing how much has been achieved. This activity can run on its own, or alongside another intervention.

Find a template online of a ladder with at least six rungs. Print out enough ladders for one child per session.

If you are working on number bond facts (for example), at the end of the intervention, go through the facts the child feels they know, writing each fact on a new rung of the ladder. This helps them establish what they have achieved, and they can take the ladder back to class/home as a reminder and prompt too.

Alternatively, you can use these to highlight facts over sessions. Write just one fact, sum, number or word per session, and use it as a review tool each time.

Teaching tip

If you use the ladders at the start of each session, they can provide a brilliant and quick revision tool.

Taking it further

Keep the ladders, or at least a copy of them, in your records to identify progress across the sessions.

#winningladders

Passing out ceremony

'I was so proud of my achievements.'

Any intervention worth its salt will take time and considerable effort from both the child and the adult, so it is important to recognise these as milestones.

Speak to the most senior line manager at your school about the need to celebrate this achievement and how it can occur. Verbal, visual and often physical recognition are all important.

Head's breakfast

This simple strategy allows the children the treat of having breakfast with the headteacher. As with all these celebratory moments, announce this to the parents or carers of the child, and take photos – this is a very media-friendly opportunity, for the price of just some juice and fresh croissants.

Golden ticket

A golden ticket for something such as 15 minutes' extra play can nevertheless be significant and a recognition of the child's achievements. Any certificate from school often ends up on the fridge door at home too, reminding them of this.

Then and now card

Similar in style to the photos used to advertise weight loss products, a laminated certificate showing written work at the start and then at the end of the intervention really highlights the difference in output, and also stands as an effective baseline of achievement (see Idea 6).

#ceremony

Maths – basic skills

Part 2

Number hunt

'I felt really important with the clipboard.'

This task takes a long time, but is about real-life maths and gives numbers a really strong context.

With your small group and a clipboard, write down three numbers they are struggling with. Ideally, all the children will have clipboards too.

Take a walk around school, seeking out numbers. You might find them on a noticeboard in the corridor or chalked onto the playground. For each number on your list, record where you saw it – and ask the children to write the number and location down too.

This activity is enormous fun and makes numbers incredibly relevant.

If numbers really are sparse around your school, use this activity as an opportunity to count with the children. For example: 'We have 4 on our list, can we find anything that is in a group of four?'

Pasta abacus

'The best lesson on addition and subtraction.'

A humble length of uncooked spaghetti is a winner with this home-made abacus. The children find manipulating beads on this so much easier than on string, and two blobs of sticky tack make this stay in one place too.

Whoever first put beads on a string to help children learn maths is a genius, and probably a very, very rich genius, as abacuses cost a fortune. This method is less flexible but it costs pennies and has other advantages over string too.

Thread ten beads onto a length of spaghetti, and secure each end with a large blob of sticky tack. Ensure that the spaghetti is long enough to slide the beads comfortably.

You have an instant line abacus. This is really easy to set up and use for all sorts of maths activities, including number bonds, simple sums, and showing greater and lesser – it really is only limited by your imagination.

You will find that a few lengths get broken at first. This is to be expected, so prepare an extra few lengths and keep them at hand – or you can show the children how to make their own.

Teaching tip

Strengthen your abacus by using three pieces of spaghetti and some hairspray.

#pastaabacus

13

Concrete manipulatives

'I can find the numbers much more easily now.'

The benefit of concrete manipulatives cannot be underestimated when it comes to interventions. There are certain tools that lend themselves to use in maths and a few more that you may not have considered. Explore these options below.

Coloured cones

These are the cones used to mark areas in PE lessons, with a big hole in the middle (reason still unknown). The cones work very well in terms of making the sharing of a number really clear. Not only does the pile reduce physically as you decrease the number, you can write a number to reveal it in the hole too. These are great for group maths, inside or outside.

Glue lids

A golden rule of primary: never throw away glue lids! Keep them in the glue tray as spares and when you have at least 11 in there, stick them to a length of strong card or wood, in a snake-like pattern, and write sequential numbers on each. You have an instant one-to-one counting snake, perfect for helping children who miss out numbers when counting.

Spacers/wedges

These are a mainstay of builders, and yet are so bright, colourful and mathematically accurate, it's incredible they haven't been bought wholesale into classrooms. Builders use these to increase beams and joists by accurate millimetres across a frame, so they are slither thin and smaller than a credit card. They are also coloured according to their heights, so can be easily sorted. I used these after a building project, where I had seemingly hundreds left over. The class loved them for maths work and they were really useful for measuring accuracy too.

Elder branches

This is an idea straight from Forest School. Have a look around the greenery in your school and find an elder tree with a spare branch. These are plants with pairs of serrated leaves and one leaf on the tip, so are quite easily identifiable. Using a school hacksaw, cut the elder branch into centimetre-long pieces, then give it to the children with a pencil and some scissors. They can poke out the soft pith in the elder branch, scrape off the bark and have fantastic counting rings as a result. These are enormously tactile, can be counted, threaded, coloured or made into bracelets or chains, and are generally lovely to use. The massive advantage of them is that they cost nothing and can be easily restocked in minutes.

Taking it further

Have the manipulatives around in the main classroom and accessible for the children, so they don't simply associate them with the intervention.

#concretemanipulatives

Compare bears

'I love using the bears and see straight away what number to use.'

This activity is great for both small group and individual interventions, and although it uses compare bears, there are a wide range of other tools you can use instead.

You can get compare bears (or counting bears) from many suppliers of maths equipment, and their uniformity allows them to be used for a variety of maths manipulative tasks in a small group. They work best in interventions, as children are often too tempted to go off-task if they are used within a whole-class situation (just like staff with fun resources during an INSET).

Instant b(e)ar chart

Using a drawn grid, with each square large enough to fit a bear, grab a handful and, one by one, place them on their own space to build up an instant bar chart of the colours you have chosen. Have the children compare the different quantities of each (have them count them up), and make comparisons, for example, 'How many more red bears are there than blue bears?'

As a progression on this, take a handful of bears and, before sorting them out, ask the children to make predictions on the different quantities. How many red bears do they think there are? How many more yellow are there than blue? By turning this raw data into a graph, it will show the children in a visible way just what a difference organising can make.

Prediction patterns (Predictabear)

With a selection of bears, line two red bears up, then follow them with a blue. Add one more red bear, and ask the children what they think will come next. Add another red, and ask again. The predictions this time are likely to be more accurate. Add another blue, and ask them what the pattern is. Some might say the pattern is RRBRRB, which is technically correct, but let them look carefully and see that this is simply RRB repeated. After other demonstrations, let them make and record their own sequences using the bears.

Time has shown that using bears when you could just use coloured cubes seems to make a difference to the participation levels and interest of the children, and this extends up into Key Stage 2.

Bonus idea ★

Use mirrors with compare bears or other one-to-one manipulatives to instantly double or halve visual support.

#comparebears

Todd and Steven's shoes

'If I ever get mixed up with odd and even, I think of pairs of shoes.'

This is a very visual intervention to help children identify the features of odd and even numbers. Although it is useful for odd and even, its benefits can pervade a wide range of maths skills.

Collect together a large range of pairs of shoes. I have found in the past that shoes for toys or small stuffed bears work best, as they don't take up too much space.

Explain that you have a friend called Todd who only has one leg. You might find it useful to have a picture of a child with just one leg. He has a friend who lives with him called Steven. Steven has two legs.

Ask them to get one pair of shoes for Steven and one shoe for Todd. How many shoes are there? The children should of course say three. Explain that Steven has an even number of feet, and every time you add an even pair of shoes, the number you have increases by two. Ask whether the number you currently have is odd or even. Do we have to add an odd or an even number of shoes to make the total odd or even?

The children quickly get the idea that two odd shoes make one even pair. This can be linked to simple algebra, by showing the equations $E + E = E$ and $E + O = O$ for example.

#oddandevenshoes

Number gravity

'Whenever I forget which way up the 6 and 9 go, I take myself through this story.'

This story is a very clear hook to help children remember number value, and it works in the same way as a memory palace. Very often, it needs just one retelling to secure it too.

'There were once two naughty balloons. They were large and shiny and shaped like the number six. One of the numbers loved the gas that filled her up so much, she sneaked over to the gas canister and took three big gulps. As quick as a flash, she popped upside down and became the number nine! Try as she might, she realised that taking those three big gulps had changed her forever!'

This is a simple enough story but, embellished the right way, sticks like mathematical glue in the children's minds. The story works best as per my original telling, when a large helium nine was donated to me by my son incredibly shortly after his ninth birthday. You can hold a helium nine as a six for much of the story, and have the children breathe in the three gulps to flip her upside down (which is actually the right way up). Canny children will also note that the nine can look like a balloon with a string, eager to float away.

Although this story is good for a whole class, it works just as well as an intervention. The children can line up magnetic numbers from one to ten, with a six at the nine space, and count along the three gulps, then turn the number over.

> **Teaching tip**
>
> Some card shops sell helium number balloons for a very reasonable price. The foil-covered numbers are best as they remain inflated for such a long time.

#floatingnumbers

Hit list

'I can do this activity in so little time, I'm in my seat before my friends sometimes.'

Any intervention out of class comes at the cost of children losing out again by virtue of them missing lesson time. A hit list solves part of this problem by being possibly the quickest intervention alive.

In this example, the five times table facts are the focus, but this could be replaced by any tables fact, tricky words – anything.

On a long strip of paper, write five facts about the five times table, without their answers. The child is extracted from the class and, just outside the door, they run through the facts as quickly as they can. They get a pencil tick for every one they get right, and a dot if they get it wrong. Three ticks and that fact has a line drawn through it, and a new fact is written below.

This occurs every day without fail. It honestly lasts less than a minute, and part of its success is down to the speed at which the task takes place. The children, similarly, love its fast pace. Try to beat the rest of the class back to their places by carrying out this intervention in the point between whole-class teaching and children returning to their seats for activities.

#hitlist

Pig islands

'I never get confused about the greater and lesser signs now.'

Although some teachers aren't keen on using the crocodiles analogy for greater and lesser signs, this neat crocodile story has an added twist — a pair of islands, with sunbathing pigs lounging around and waiting to be eaten!

On the board, draw two hills, one to the left and the other to the right. Ensure that there is enough space to write a number in each hill. Explain that these are the twin Pig Islands, occupied only by sunbathing pigs. It is a fairly dreamlike existence for the pigs, apart from one small problem — the crocodile who loves to eat pigs. Because he is a lazy crocodile, he will only ambush the beach with the most pigs on it.

Write '3' on the left island, and '8' on the other. Which is the larger number? The children in your group should identify '8' as being larger (if not, get some maths equipment out). Explain that the crocodile will attack this island first because it has more pigs. Draw the 'less than' symbol so that the children can see that the crocodile's jaws are open towards the larger number. Explain why this is again.

Wipe the jaws and numbers away, then put a larger number on the left island, and repeat, several times. The children pick up on this enormously quickly and can't wait to join in!

In a short space of time, you'll be able to draw the crocodile's jaws open one way, and have children say a number of pigs on each island. Talk through the equation every time or have the children discuss it in pairs.

Teaching tip

This really needs to be drawn out to get the full effect. Don't go to a generic teaching website — the children will think you are an artist if you draw it yourself.

#pigisland

Timeline tasks

'This has helped me organise myself.'

Time can be a very tricky concept for a child to operate internally. This activity helps secure this more firmly.

Prepare some blank watch templates (complete with faces and straps) for the children you are working with to write upon. Ensure there is enough space for this.

Talk to the children about what they did to get ready for school in the morning. Write each of these activities down on one of the watch straps.

When this is done, order these with the children to ensure there is a proper sequence. Talk about what sort of time they get up, and write this in the first watch face (either analogue or digital), and then continue with each event, updating the time that each event occurs.

Talk through the chronology of the times and events, then mix the watch straps up and have the child reorder them, naming the time and event for each strap.

String lengths

'This is a really practical way of measuring.'

Have you ever taught a child who, when they work on number bonds to ten, simply cannot see the patterns? If so, this simple intervention is for you and it works with string, wool, ribbon — even strawberry laces!

Find some uneven lengths of string, wool or ribbon, and cut them into 10cm lengths. If this seems too small for the children to manipulate, use 20cm lengths, and remember that you will have to use 2cm increments.

With the group, explain that you have some 10 unit lengths of string. Make a big show of clearing the space, marking 10cm on the table (writing on the table with a whiteboard pen gets the BEST kind of gasp), and cut 1cm along the one length you have in front of you.

Demonstrate that 9 is not 10, 1 is not 10, but that both 1 + 9 makes 10 and 9 + 1 makes 10. Have them prove it to you. Do the same for the rest of the number bonds, talking through it and testing the children on it each time.

Experiment with how you can make 10 with two or three lengths together. Check each time against the line you have made. This will cement understanding for many children in your group.

Teaching tip

Keeping these lengths for another time you are covering number bonds is incredibly helpful.

#stringlengths

Puzzle hackers

'Word problems make so much more sense now.'

Using these small techniques together can make the difference between a child who cannot fathom a word problem and one who knows exactly what steps to take in order to turn the jumble of words into an equation.

This activity requires you to print out word problems as large as you can make them. Find a variety of styles but all a year or so lower than the level the children are currently working at – we are teaching the principles of unpacking a problem, not the maths itself, so they should feel success from solving the former.

Start with a vocal reading of the problem. Read it aloud, asking the children to indicate every time they hear a maths term or a number used.

Do this again, but this time with a highlighter. Support the children in highlighting the key terms and numbers.

Fishing time – sometimes maths problems use numbers that aren't relevant to trick us. We call these red herrings. Explain this to the children and use a red pen to circle them. This is really important to check through, even if there aren't any present.

Next we draw an equals sign and a box. Reading the question again, work out together what sort of answer the question wants. Is it a number, a price, a length in centimetres, the number of girls on the rugby team? Define the answer and write this down too.

Only now is the time to identify the equation type. Draw the four symbols at the top, and refresh everyone on what they are called and what they do to a number (additions make things larger and so on). With their eagle eyes, can the children find the word or phrase that best identifies what type of equation the sum is? Have them find the word and repeat it to you.

Finally, write out the raw equation. It should draw on all the facts and numbers given in the problem. Explain clearly how the words have been reduced to an equation.

Solve the equation, and check back that the answer makes sense – if we have 10.5 as the number of girls on the rugby team, does this make sense?

Taking it further

There is no acronym for Read, Highlight, Fish, Answer, Equation, Check, so have these words on a sticky note nearby to prompt you (and them) instead.

#puzzlehackers

Shape sort

'I love this game; it doesn't feel like work at all!'

With very little preparation, this intervention can be passed to a teaching assistant for a quick revision session as the need arises. Shapes can be notoriously difficult to recall for some children, and this resolves many issues quickly.

Teaching tip

Use an exotic bag if you can find one to make the activity more desirable. Make the bag one they will covet.

Find a suitable bag that can hold a variety of 2D shapes. Bring this bag out in front of the group of children you're working with, and say that you have selected a shape inside the bag. You can only answer 'yes' or 'no' to the questions they give, and they can only ask whether it is a shape of a specific name after five questions. You can select a shape by putting your hand in the bag or feeling the shape from outside the bag.

The children may start by asking how many sides it has, which you can't answer. This can lead to questions such as 'does it have an even number of sides?' or the even more refined 'does it have more than three sides?'

Every time the children ask a question, make a big show of checking what they have asked. For example, if they ask whether the shape has four sides, be seen to silently count the sides before answering 'yes' or 'no'.

Taking it further

This works just as well with older children needing to learn more complex or 3D shapes.

You'll notice how quickly they become accustomed to identifying the shapes.

It is really interesting to hear the questions that don't actually help us; asking, for example, if the shape is red does not help us to identify the shape itself. It may be worth writing down these 'red herring' questions on sticky notes, so the children know not to ask them again.

#shapebag

English – spelling, word types and punctuation

Part 3

BeD time

'I finally get the difference and don't mix them up anymore.'

One of the most common letter transpositions is that of b and d, and this simple little set of interventions will help to lock in the difference. It has a handy physical mnemonic too!

Teaching tip

Teach the whole class the physical mnemonic – they'll end up reminding each other.

The letters b and d are very often mixed up and transposed by children, seemingly up to the end of junior school. This is a really easy one to solve, using the simple strategies outlined below.

Hand gestures

Put your hands in front of you as if holding a box. Close up all of the fingers except for the pointing fingers and thumb, and make a ring with each of these then raise the middle fingers. You have made the word bed, with b on the left-hand side, d on the right. Children love using this hand gesture mnemonic in order to remember that b looks like the b of bed and d looks like the d of bed, as your hands have shown.

Spot the odd ones out

Having a sheet of 'b's and 'd's, written in a variety of sizes and fonts is a brilliant way of getting the children to read and check their own corrections. Simply move your pencil underneath the letters, having the child say what letter it is that you are pointing to. Circle the ones they get wrong. Doing a page of this every single day can, over a very short space of time, help the child to recognise the correct letter formation.

Alphabetical

Having an alphabet displayed in the classroom is often taken as default, without the true benefit of it being used. Put an arrow under the b and the d, and every time there is a mistake ask the children to identify which letter it should be. They will soon recognise that b comes before d in the alphabet.

#BeDtime

Vowel play

'I know all the vowels now!'

Nailing into the subconscious all of the vowels is pretty key early on, and if this isn't in place, lots of other spelling work can be hampered. This intervention works with all ages.

With the children and a large piece of paper, draw around one outstretched hand. Get an apple, and place it on the thumb. What is this? What is the first sound the word makes? Ask the children to write an 'a' on their drawn thumb. Ask the children what the next vowel is, and place an egg on the first finger of your model and demonstrate to them how to draw an 'e'. Repeat this with all the vowels, then you can start playing!

Hide
The children cover their eyes. You remove an item, then the children open their eyes, and say the letter that corresponds to the missing item (not the missing item itself). They will begin by checking their card hand at first (which is fine, as it's supporting their understanding).

Hand letters
Children put their hands over their card outline, point to a finger and say the letter. They should do this repeatedly, then challenge each other.

Show me
Hands behind backs. You say a vowel, and they have to quickly show you the finger or thumb associated with that letter.

CVC gloves
With some consonant cubes, the card outlines can be used. Simply put some cubes out, and have the children experiment with making CVC (consonant – vowel – consonant) words. Can the CVC sequence work with all the vowels? What if the consonants were reversed? Which are the best letters to use?

Teaching tip

This intervention works best with physical props for all the vowels where possible. Collect an apple, egg, ice cube (a Perspex® cube works just as well), an Oreo (or an orange) and a cocktail umbrella (endless fun).

Taking it further

Let the children draw the objects on their paper hands if you think it will help (although sometimes the pictures can be a little less representative).

#vowelplay

Spelling keepie-uppie

'I know that the wrong answer leads to help, which helps me learn.'

Invented by my brilliant teaching assistant (TA), Shirley Chiwera, who saw a need that I had overlooked, this strategy takes spelling tests to a much more comfortable end point than simply a poor score.

Teaching tip

Good record keeping is the key here – make this as simple as possible and persuade your TA to track EVERYTHING.

Taking it further

The philosophy of 'a wrong answer tells you more than a right answer' pervades all good teaching and feedback but it is never more true than in this technique.

#spellingtracker

After the weekly spelling test, collect in all the test papers and order them from lowest mark to highest mark. Using a spare spelling sheet, write down the names of the children who got zero at the top, those who scored one next to '1', and so on, until you have six names. Leave this paper and the spelling test papers in the TA tray (an essential piece of kit) to pick up the next day. They need only practise the words the children got wrong (for those who got none correct, set more appropriate words).

My TA used to record the children on the list each week, so we could keep track of those who were finding specific word groupings or spellings in general tricky.

This may seem obvious, but this monitoring of spellings simply isn't done enough.

Spelling rainbows

'I hardly ever forget the letters now.'

Seven colours and a large word are all you need to help train the children in learning the shape of words they find tricky.

Prepare a large sheet of paper, a range of coloured pens and a black pen. Print a simple word on the paper using the black pen. Talk to the children about the shape the word makes, and how the descenders and ascenders operate.

Using the red pen, draw a boundary line around the shape, talking about whichever letter you are currently going around as you form this new shape.

Next get the orange pen and repeat. Continue until you have used all seven colours. You should still be able to distinguish the outline of the words and the shapes that individual letters form.

Write a simple learning word with the children on their paper, and have them repeat the task with their word. Ensure they continue the running commentary of the letter they are outlining as they go.

Teaching tip

Richard Of York Gave Battle In Vain is both a fact and an easy mnemonic to help remember the colours and order of the rainbow.

#spellingrainbow

Word grids

'I can read the words really well that I couldn't before.'

Word grids take seconds to prepare and can help children who know all the letters in a word, but not necessarily the right order.

Make some blank grids in your word processing program – three-by-three grids, with enough space to write words in each box, would be best. Either laminate these sheets or put them in a clear plastic wallet.

On the grid, write the word the child is struggling with (in this case, 'like') three times. Fill the grid with other words. For an easier task, write down completely different words such as 'mum' and 'boy'. For a harder task, and one more likely to have greater impact, fill it with similar words such as 'look' as well as misspellings of the base word, such as 'leik' and 'leki'.

There are two ways to play this. The first is to use counters and ask the child to cover up EITHER the words that are correct or (and better) the words that aren't correct.

The other way to play this game is to write the words on the laminated grid in board pen and have the child wipe away the wrong words. They LOVE wiping away the teacher's writing!

#wordgrid

Popcorn words

'Sorting and learning – and POPCORN.'

Your children will love sorting the words into different categories, and plastic popcorn containers can be picked up for next to nothing – and be written on in board marker too.

Write 'Noun', 'Verb' and 'Adjective' on each of the popcorn containers. Using small slips of paper, write a few examples of each, scrunch them up and put them in the wrong containers.

With the children now present, explain that they are making word popcorn, and that these pieces of popcorn have been mixed up.

Pour out the popcorn from the containers and unwrap one, reading it to the group. They will tell you which container to put it into. Scrunch it back up and put it into the right container. Have them sort the rest of the words into the correct categories, then make their own popcorn for the containers.

At the end, give each child a container to check all the words are correct.

#popcornwords

Looking sheepish

'My teacher has this on a poster in the class, so I can always check what I need to put.'

This is the best type of activity — your class will be so keen to complete this chart of singular and plural for you, while at the same time preparing a fantastic intervention activity.

Teaching tip

I love breaking these categories down further by saying that some of the words in the 'MANY' column are linked in some way. Lead them to identify matching suffixes (-s or -es) for example, and have them either think of others or sort the ones available.

Taking it further

This obviously lends itself perfectly well to extending with ownership. Turn the table into a Carroll diagram with an extra line and share our ownership to 'one' and 'many'. This can help with demonstrating those tricky nouns whose singular and plural are the same (such as sheep), as they will sit in the intersection.

#sheepish

Find some large coloured paper (sometimes called sugar paper for some unexplained reason) and turn it into a landscape, two-column chart. Either write 'ONE' at the top of the left column and 'MANY' on the other, or draw a smiley face on the left and a smiley face plus the addition sign on the other.

Give out a few sticky notes to each child and ensure they have access to pencils or pens.

Ask them to choose an object in the classroom and tell you what it is. Write down that word as a singular noun and put it in the left column. Ask them for another object, pluralise it and put that in the right column. Do this several times until they pick up on what 'one' and 'many' (or the smiley faces) refer to. The best way to test this is to put a word in the wrong column deliberately. If they understand, you'll receive some loud protests!

Have the children think about items in their bedroom and ask them to write one in each column. You'll instantly have a full display to talk about with the children.

This may seem like a very obvious skill but you will find that making this categorisation visual provides a really effective hook for the children.

Contraction bricks

'I finally understand how contractions are built.'

These require a little preparation but the children will love using them. They explain in a very visual way how contractions work and which ones go together.

Group up three bricks – two small and one large – that fit together to make a solid wall of the same length. The two small bricks should sit atop the one large brick.

On the top bricks, write down the two root words that make a contraction, for example CAN NOT. On the lower, larger brick, write down the contraction itself – CAN'T.

Repeat for all the contractions you want to cover.

You now have a complete set of contraction bricks. These can be used in a variety of ways:

- Match up the long- and short-form contractions.
- Mix up the long-form contractions – which work and which don't?
- With paper underneath, identify what has been taken away from the contraction to make it so.

These bricks are worth the time spent making them, as they can be used to sit on the desks of those children who consistently mix up contractions or don't even remember to use them.

#contractionbricks

The fullest stop

'I hardly ever forget full stops now and when I do, my friend helps me out.'

Younger children tend to fall into two camps when learning full stops — they either forget to use them or create lead meteorite holes in their paper! This is a set of ideas to help with the most reluctant of punctuation marks (for some) — the full stop.

Gather together the three currencies for full stops. I have found over time that bow pasta, sticky tack and LEGO® heads work brilliantly. Two of these are expensive but that is almost the point of using them as opposed to beads or something of that size.

Put the currencies in cups or pots, and with your group, ask them to write a sentence. At the end of every sentence, tell them that if they forget to leave a larger-than-normal space, they get a bow tie shape, if they put the full stops at the end of all their writing, they get a blob of sticky tack and if they remember the full stop and space as they go, they get a LEGO® head. These are all placed on the full stops as you go (or at the end).

You will quickly notice how focused on the full stops the children become and they are incredibly keen to get as many LEGO® heads on their work as possible!

At the end, tally up how many of each they get, and note this down for next time. At the start of the next session or writing task, remind them of their habit (either no space, no full stop, or putting them all in at the end) and challenge them to get a better score this time.

#bigfullstops

Speech mark comics

'If it's in a bubble, it's in speech mark trouble.'

The use of comic strips to help children learn the difference between direct and indirect speech remains elusive as a panacea to this challenge, yet with the right guidance, this simple skill practice can transform the confidence of some children.

Collect together a range of comic strips, both with text in the bubbles and blank strips. My love for Calvin and Hobbes extends enough to use them for this activity; the humour is understood and loved by Year 3 upwards.

Start by highlighting each character's speech in a different colour. Go through the rules for direct speech with the children, especially 'new speaker, new line'. Write out with them (or have prepared) the actual words said. Put the direct speech marks on first, then add the verbs and nouns afterwards. Emphasise that only what is in the bubbles is surrounded by speech marks.

Have the children fill in the speech for an 'empty bubble' strip, then do the same again. You will be surprised by the number of children who actually get this technique already.

Repeat as necessary. Sticking the strips into their writing books, then writing the prose underneath really helps the children to lock in the rule and also provides a good place to check back at a later date if they get stuck.

Teaching tip

Search online for blank comic strips or comic frames – don't spend hours making these yourself!

Taking it further

You can now get sticky notes that look like speech bubbles. Low budget? Find a speech bubble shape on your word processor, then print it onto sticky labels.

#speechmarkcomics

English – reading for expression

Part 4

Watch me

'I can pronounce all my words correctly now.'

It is surprising how few interventions make explicit use of vocal modelling — watching how something is pronounced and said. This small skill will help with recognition, expression and even spelling.

If you are working on a new letter, sound or number, take 30 seconds for the child to watch as you pronounce it slowly. Ask them to observe the way your lips and tongue move together to make the sound. Have them put their hand just below their own chin to feel the number of syllables a word has.

Have them repeat the task to you, pointing out exactly what they need to do to make it perfect. Often, adults miss out this explicit guidance but watching someone do this makes all the difference.

This is particularly important with phonics. Watch an early years foundation stage (EYFS) teacher for a real insight into vocal modelling — they are the true experts at this. It is used far less in Year 6 interventions, at great cost. If you doubt this, observe what you do next time someone introduces themselves and they have an unusual name. Your eyes will focus on their faces (particularly their mouth) as you repeat the name back to them. Do this for all unfamiliar words and you will notice great progression in a short space of time.

#watchme

Blending hoops

'It's so easy to see how the letters blend now.'

Hoops from the PE cupboard can work so well in the classroom too. This activity uses them to help children with blending letters together.

Collect together as many forms of the letters T and H as you can and have two hoops ready, sitting side by side.

Mix up the letters in a line and have the child you are working with push them upwards, one at a time, saying the sound they make each time (not the name of the letter).

Once this is completed correctly, ask the child to sort the letters so that the Ts all go in the left-hand hoop, and the Hs in the right-hand loop. Offer support as necessary.

Overlap the hoops and ask what could go in the middle section. Demonstrate this by taking one T and one H, and blending them together in the middle. Have the child repeat this, sounding out the new sound as they go.

This works for all combinations of blended sounds, and with three hoops, you can form trigraphs too.

Teaching tip

If you don't have the working space to use hoops, draw two intersecting circles on large paper. Hoops work as a really good visual cue though.

Taking it further

This is a perfect way of introducing more ways to use Venn diagrams with the children (remembering that the way the Venn is used here doesn't strictly follow Venn diagram rules).

#blendinghoops

Megaphone reading

'I've never had so much fun reading to others.'

This is the type of intervention that will initially make some senior leaders worry that something has gone wrong – but they won't be further from the truth.

Taking it further

This activity also works brilliantly for those confident readers who don't show expression when reading. Model this for the children first.

Gather the children you are working with together (this works best with three or four), along with some of their recent work. It should ideally be some prose of at least ten sentences. It can be a text you would like them to read, but the real purpose of this intervention is to get the children reading some of their own work, since that is possibly the hardest task to do.

Have the children stand in the middle of the school hall, playground or field in a triangle. They take it in turns to read a sentence, going clockwise. Every time they can hear the sentence clearly, they take one step back from the triangle. Every time they can't hear the sentence clearly, they take a step forward.

Before long, you'll have three timid children shouting their sentences clearly to the other two and physically seeing the impact of their clarity.

Upgrade this activity by having the children start again, but this time ask them to use their most expressive voices. The same rules about moving forward and backward apply.

#megaphonereading

Nonsense news report

'Reading has never been this much fun!'

Tablets can be used for a great many things but an autocue is one of the best!

Find a few stories to cut and paste from a children's news website and make very deliberate changes to the story – instead of a man going into space, for example, make it an angry troll.

Put these stories into a 'notes' app on a tablet, and then explain to the children that they are news reporters and will have to read whatever they see on the screen as if it is a serious news report. This activity works best if they have no idea of what will appear on the screen.

Sit them behind a desk and slowly scroll the text up as they read. Encourage great expression and reactions as they read, and practise several times.

In reality, the children are simply reading, but the change of content and context brings out a new element of reading for some. This is an activity they will want to repeat again and again. Have them 'practise' by reading their story books in the same way.

Taking it further

If you have another tablet to hand, record the children's broadcast and play it back to the class. They will be held in high esteem by their classmates for doing this and you will have definitive evidence of expressive reading to show them and their parents or to publish on the school website.

#nonsensenews

Luncherature

'We love our lunch readers.'

Want to tackle the confidence of readers AND the high ambient noise of infant lunches? Try combining the two!

#luncherature

The research is clear: children make progress in reading when they hear books read aloud.

One quick and sustained way to gain traction with reading from older pupils is to introduce luncherature. This is a concept whereby older children read stories to younger children as they eat their lunch.

The benefits are manifold – the children are generally quieter, eat slightly more slowly and are exposed to more literature than they might be used to. For the reader, they learn to read with purpose and expression, to a very excited and willing audience.

Although there may be a temptation to use short storybooks, larger chapter books, where the plots and characters are sustained over several days or weeks, tend to be more effective. Author Jim Trelease recommends that books three years above the child's reading levels are perfect for reading aloud to them.

Chain reading

'I never know when I'm reading next so I keep track of where I am.'

Chain reading is actually the opposite of following a chain. We all have moments in group reading where people lose their place due to inattention. This resolves that problem at a stroke.

This activity works best in a small group of up to six readers. You need to either know all your readers or ensure they all have name labels, as you will use their names several times.

Explain that you are going to read a passage twice. You will start, and you will then say a name, and that person must read on from this point until a new name is said.

Reading in this way ensures that everyone stays on their toes the whole time, listening carefully to the reader, as they don't know when it will be their turn next.

Mix up the order in which you say the names – any pattern will do, just avoid going clockwise or anti-clockwise. Skipping every other child seems to appear random enough not to get picked up on by children.

Teaching tip

Have one of the children decide who should read next. They love this responsibility (aka POWER).

Taking it further

Take this intervention as a whole class so that all children are equipped with the same skills.

#chainreading

Seesaw reading

'This has helped me so much in concentrating on what I am going to read next.'

Modelling is best done just before the children try something for themselves and seesaw reading really does close the gap when doing this.

Teaching tip

Discuss afterwards the different ways in which you were reading and how it varied from how the children read normally.

Taking it further

To help them gain independence, have a confident child become the reading leader and have them model to the others how to read.

#seesawreading

Set out the reading group so that they are comfortable and all have access to the book. Ensure that they know what is going to happen next. You are going to read one physical line of the text you are studying and, together, they are going to read the next line.

Emphasise how important it is to ensure that they are reading with the same speed, cadence and flow as you have just modelled.

The children respond enormously well to this activity and you can also introduce different elements of expression depending on the genre.

English – reading for meaning

Part 5

Text detectives

'I feel I can find out more from a text than I did before.'

Posing questions is one of the most powerful ways of building up information about something you are studying. This task extends this even further but is very time-intensive, making it perfect for an intervention.

#textdetectives

Prepare a children's news report, printed in large font on A4 sheets. Brainstorm with the children the 'Five Big W Questions' – 'Who', 'What', 'Where', 'When' and 'Why' – and write these separately on sticky notes, scattered in a large circle on the table in front of you.

You can either have the children read the passage to themselves, then write down the salient facts for each question, or they can cut out the individual elements and gather them next to the correct sticky note.

When complete, hide the original text and have them retell you the story, turning over each sticky note or cut-out fact as they mention it. This really helps to highlight what they have and haven't covered.

Federal Bureau of Inference

'It made me look more carefully at a text I'd read a few times but not seen all the clues.'

This idea frames texts as being like an investigation and helps to ensure children are joining known facts together to gain inferred facts.

Use a template that has two small boxes with an addition sign between them, followed by an equals sign and then a larger box. In faint shading, have 'fact' written in the two smaller boxes and 'inference' written in the larger box. You will then have an inference equation.

Explain to the children that in many books, some things are written (facts) while other things are alluded to (inferences). Use the following sentence to help explain this principle:

'Amy shivered outside on the snowy day.'

Model looking at the sentence and writing down the equation words in the blank boxes:

SHIVERED + SNOWY = Amy is cold

Help the children to find and write down other examples in the chosen text.

Taking it further

I have found that laminating the equation strips and having them available during text analysis helps to focus some children's detective skills.

#fbischool

The story so far

'I'm much better at remembering key details now.'

While the prologue to *Star Wars* explains the backstory in diminishing text, far more effective is a recap of 'the story so far' by your group, as you read through a story.

This activity works best with a long-form fiction book rather than a picture book. Before each reading session, ask the children three questions about the text.

What is the story so far?

Offer up prompts rather than questions when eliciting the answers to this question. You ideally want the children to give a strong answer to the question, with character names, plots and plot arcs. Make visual notes of details as the group gives you the story so far.

What might happen next?

This is an opportunity for children to come up with some sensible predictions about future happening events. Ask them why they think that this or that might be the case, and try to get them to draw from the existing text rather than random guesswork, which will be vague and less likely to occur.

What is missing?

This question is deliberately vague, and encourages a deeper use of compare and contrast skills with the group. What is missing could be a puzzle that hasn't been answered, a criticism of the text itself (such as there is no character we feel sympathy for) or even something clear (such as no narration). This offers the teacher a chance to unpick views with ease but can take a while to develop with children.

#storysofar

Story jigsaws

'I love these stories!'

This is an idea for developing readers that is so stunningly effective, I'm amazed it took so long to think up! Imagine a choose-your-own-adventure story, but with a fun twist — none of the alternative stories are related!

Find six short stories, which are around one page each in the same font. Prepare them so that there is a healthy space between paragraphs, then slice and laminate the strips. Mix them up and put them in a zippy pocket for the session.

Explain that you have six stories, split up by paragraphs and mixed up. The children have to rebuild the stories as efficiently as possible.

This task requires conversation, discussion, disagreement and deduction. You will find that the children read the story extracts far more quickly than they might do normally, since there is a purpose behind their reading.

You may notice that the children skim-read the extracts and simply look for clues (such as the same name appearing repeatedly) — this is a key skill and should be encouraged. Given the same challenge, it is probably what most adults would do too.

Teaching tip

These take some preparation and so they are ripe for the lamination treatment. If you are going to use it more than once, trap it in plastic!

Taking it further

If you want a real challenge, tell the children there are five stories or even seven! This will help them to distinguish between the stories and correctly identify that there are actually six.

#storyjigsaws

Take note

'I love looking back at the story notes my adult helper has made.'

Borrowed wholesale from teaching colleague Louise Parsons at Riverbridge Primary School in Staines, this is a picture book, made by the teaching assistant (TA) and the child they are supporting, and created while the whole-class story is being read. It is phenomenal in its simplicity and effectiveness, and you can use it in your class right away.

Teaching tip

Add a date and page number at the start and end of each section for reference.

This is a long-burn task, but utilises your class TA and is especially effective when you are reading a book and want all the class in on the story, so don't want anyone taken out for intervention.

Using an A5 wide-ruled book, the TA sits with the child or children who most need supportive input when a story is being read.

The traditional method of supporting this child is to write or draw on a whiteboard, but this loses any permanency of the recording. Instead, the TA and child co-construct their version of the story in the lined book as it proceeds.

This can be in the form of words, diagrams, doodles, pictures, even character descriptions and keywords that may be helpful.

The child (and the TA) can then draw on this when they are working, and it can provide helpful prompts and ideas for both parties.

These end up being brilliant books of recordings and thoughts, as well as a ready resource for other students.

#takenote

Tracking tools

'I love my superhero pointer.'

Following words as you read is fundamental as a reader. Here are some different approaches you can take to help children with this key skill.

Ruler or card strip

A ruler or a strip of card is very useful as a tracking device for children who tend to jump ahead. Remember to only cover up subsequent sentences – show the entire sentence the child is reading, not just the actual line they are working on.

Pointing fingers

This can be either the child's own finger or a cardboard finger (which can also be a finger-space device). Encourage a moving finger rather than one that is staccato for each word, to improve flow.

Decorated lollipop stick

This idea is an absolute winner with children who struggle with finger tracking. Get a lollipop stick and decorate the stick with the topic theme, such as a superhero, or with whatever will interest the child. This of course can double up as a bookmark.

Reading eyes

This is a concept rather than something physical and is the position you want to get to – the child is tracking words with their eyes and not a tool. It is helpful to have the term to use, so that the children remember to use their eyes rather than their fingers.

Teaching tip

Never cover the pictures in a book – they are essential for understanding.

Taking it further

If a child who is a good reader starts skipping words, it is often because they have transitioned to reading ahead of what they are reading aloud. This is a normal and natural process, and often means you should let them read silently for a little while to adjust to this new reading format.

#trackingtools

Word fishing

'I love fishing for words.'

There are several distinct stages to reading words, the most essential being reading words in context. If you have a child who is excellent at reading words in isolation, but struggles with words in the text, this activity is perfect.

The preparation for this requires some creative writing. Type out the five keywords you want to focus on across the top of the page. Below this list, write a short story, trying to feature each of these words at least three times. It doesn't have to be anything brilliant, more functional, so don't get hung up on how successful the writing is.

With the child and a highlighter, read through the five keywords together, then start the timer. The child has to read through and find all of the keywords within the text as quickly as possible. To score the point, they need to highlight them and read them aloud.

Stop the timer when they have finished and record the time.

Carry this activity out several times, perhaps even using different fonts, to improve the personal score of the child.

Teaching tip

Laminate the text and use a board pen to help retain resources.

Taking it further

As an extension, remove the keywords, leaving an underline, a blank or a shaded box, and have the child work out which words go in the spaces. This will obviously take longer, but will help establish whether the child knows what the words mean.

#wordfishing

Gap reading

'I love leaping into the gap.'

Help the children keep up with reading aloud with this simple game they will love. It will transform how well they follow the text you are reading together.

This is a really easy concept to grasp and helps with stopping children from drifting when you read together.

With the text in front of everyone in your group, explain that you will be reading and everyone else will be following with their finger. At certain points, you will miss out a word and they are all to read it aloud, mirroring your speed, tone and expression.

Start by missing out simple words and build up to words that are challenging or unusual. This is a great teaching opportunity to pick up on expanded vocabulary.

Teaching tip

Don't let this be an activity you only do with poor readers – it is a great task to use with the more able children too.

Taking it further

Vary the challenge by asking the children to come up with a synonym for the word you miss out as quickly as they can. This produces a rich range of words and can also identify some vocabulary confusion too.

#gapreading

Quadrant thinking

'We all felt like we'd helped to solve the problem together.'

Having four perspectives on one problem can help develop thinking strategies. The children love using quadrant sheets — they take seconds to make, yet engage all learners. This is a version of an idea seen on Twitter, source unknown.

Either fold a sheet of A3 into quarters diagonally or draw two lines diagonally across the page. Put one of the following four titles in each space: 'Queries', 'Qualities', 'Predictions' and 'Puzzles'. In the middle of the page, add the source. This can be a word problem, a text extract or even a statement.

With the children positioned around the sheet so there is one child facing each quadrant, have them look at the source, and then write in their quadrant their response to it in relation to the area defined.

Queries: questions they may have about the source.

Qualities: elements or things they have learnt from the source.

Predictions: what they think the answer will be/what happens next/what they think their task will be.

Puzzles: elements about the source that don't make sense.

Rotate the sheet when everyone has contributed to their section, until every child has contributed to every quadrant.

You will find that what some children write down will inspire and generate ideas for other quadrants.

#quadrantthinking

English – supporting reluctant readers

Part 6

Sentence bargains

'I have read so much.'

This really is the silver bullet activity for reluctant readers and takes absolutely no preparation or resources — just an upbeat approach and the ability to be competitive with the child you are working with.

We all have a reluctant reader in class and their desire to read is always outweighed by their hope that you will read to them. Flip this positively by opening their book and counting the words in a sentence. Bet with them that the child won't be able to read, say, half the words.

Of course, you aren't trying to diminish their confidence or ability to read; you will support, prompt and coax as normal, and give them the benefit of the doubt.

This sounds like it shouldn't work but it really does. Once you have been successful with one sentence, up the ante by asking them to read one more word than they did before in the next sentence. They will jump on the chance to 'beat the adult' and soon be begging to read all the words in a sentence.

Taking it further

Keeping a tally score of wins motivates the children no end and adds some maths in too.

#sentencebargains

Genre boxes

'I love knowing which box to choose my books from.'

This task is highly creative and will add artistic flair to your class book corner. It also shakes off the shackles of the painful reading ladder of books sorted by colour band.

Collect together some children's shoe boxes and a wide range of craft materials – go all out if you can.

Have a wide range of books from your current scheme in front of you and make sure they are from a collection of book bands. Reintroduce the concept of genres to the children and redefine them as necessary. Write the genres on separate sheets of paper.

Start categorising the books you have by the genres, adding to the genre list as appropriate.

Choose one genre and explain that the books will now be kept in genre boxes. Talk about a specific example and model ideas of how the box might be designed. For example:

Spy – Dress up the box in a long brown coat, sunglasses or a newspaper with eyeholes cut out.

Medieval – Turn the box into a castle with toilet roll turrets and tiny flags.

With the children, come up with genre designs for each box and set to work. This might be a project to work on with a small group each afternoon for a week if the timetable allows.

The children involved will burst with pride seeing their boxes used by the whole class and you will also introduce the children to new books they might not have considered reading beforehand.

Teaching tip

The colour banding can still work but this activity will offer a different incentive to some children on a lower band to want to achieve more.

#genreboxes

Morning challenges

'I am so much more organised in the morning now.'

We all have the child who, while everyone else is reading first thing in the morning, is busy wandering around the classroom. This simple activity sets the child up to succeed with ease.

Create a 3 x 4 grid and fill half of the boxes with quick wins for your wandering reader. These could be:

- bag away
- sitting down
- book open
- diary open
- looking at book
- one line read
- one page read.

Laminate this card and tape it to the child's desk. In your morning movements around the classroom, keep coming back to them and tick all that they have achieved. You'll note that they get a third of their boxes ticked just by being set up to read.

Challenge them to get to the end of the boxes – to get everything ticked off – by the time you start the register.

Debugging a book

'I understand the book I'm reading so much better now.'

How often do we give a child their next reading book without even unpicking it? Worse still, tell the child to pick their next book from the same book band? This activity takes a little time but it front-loads interest and excitement in the child.

Marie Clay, doyenne of early reading skills, came up with the phrase 'debugging a book': taking a book apart so that it is more accessible for the reader. I recommend that you take the 'debugging' steps below with all books read by struggling or reluctant readers.

Teaching tip

Each 'debug' takes precious minutes away from hearing a child read, but it is enormously valuable. Try it with a few readers to see the difference.

Preparation
Read through the book yourself. Consider questions you could ask the child about the theme or topic. Decide if the book has an interesting key point to hold back.

The cover
Read the cover to the child. Ask them what they think the book is about and explain that it is an x book about some characters called y and z.

Tell the book
Explain the basic story as you turn the pages with the child. Look at the pictures and point out key characters, objects, etc. Respond to any questions as you go along.

Stop at a hook point
If there is a dramatic ending, hold back these pages and ask the child what they think will happen next. This is done to raise the child's desire to find out more.

Ask for feedback
A crucial step – ask the child if they think they will enjoy the book and why. Too often we give children their next book without finding out what they thought of the last one.

#debugabook

English – writing

Part 7

Play dough dictionary

'I love using the play dough for letters and words.'

You can make non-edible play dough for use in class in minutes (see the teaching tip for a simple recipe) and it will make such a difference in helping children form their letters for tricky words.

Take a lump of play dough out of the container and roll it into an upright shape. Ask the children what it looks like. They will say a '1' or an 'l'. Ask the children what we could add to this 'l' to make other letters in the alphabet. They should, perhaps with some prompting, suggest t, p, h, j, k, d, b.

Have the children make these letters, looking at what has been added or removed each time. If you have enough play dough (note, there is no such thing as too much play dough), keep all the letters, so that children can see the differences side by side.

Build up these skills by forming other letters.

This also works well for numbers: you can make the numbers, then make little play dough balls and place them on the number – three on the number three, and so on.

You can use Numicon to act as a cookie template with play dough too. Used carefully, with a level amount in each space, you can merge the cookies to show that six is greater than two, for example.

Taking it further

Make play dough one lunchtime in the staffroom – it is wonderfully stress-relieving to knead the dough and you'll have some help from your colleagues too!

#playdoughletters

Ice cube CVC

'I made lots of words really quickly.'

This activity is quick and easy to set up, especially if you have an ice cube tray with three rows large enough to have magnetic letters sitting in each individual compartment.

Position the ice cube tray in front of the child 'portrait' style and give them a pile of letters, laid flat, the right way up. Ask the child to make a CVC (consonant – vowel – consonant) word. Place these letters in the top row. Demonstrate that the vowel always sits in the middle.

Ask the children to choose a vowel and place it in the middle of the next row. See if they can find two consonants to place either side. Help them with the last letter, as this is the one they are most likely to struggle with at first.

Repeat until the tray is full. Using their 'reading eyes' (see Idea 43) have them read back the CVC words to you from top to bottom. Next, say each word and have them point it out to you. This encourages them to read through all the words.

Finally, ask them to take a CVC word out of the tray carefully, lay it out on the table and read it out.

Teaching tip

Place a vowel upright in the compartment right in the middle of the tray and stick it down with tape. Then, either randomly scoop out magnetic letters to see if any CVC words are formed (or can be adjusted) or place one letter in the left-hand side and have the children find a letter for the right-hand side.

Taking it further

Write C, V and C in each of the sections to assist those who are still struggling.

#icecubeCVC

Alien words

'I love making up alien words.'

You might not like or even approve of the concept of alien words but children adore them. Utilise this enthusiasm by letting them generate whole villages of aliens, while sifting out any real words discovered en route.

Teaching tip

See Idea 95 for more activities with magnetic letters.

You will need a page of colourful aliens to name – these can be found by searching online for a whole host of cartoon aliens to copy and print out for their naming ceremony.

With the magnetic letters, ask each child in your group to make a CVC (consonant – vowel – consonant) word to be used as a root word. Tell them you are seeking out alien names and they can make them by adding or replacing one letter at a time in their root word. Have them slide away the letter they don't want (making the sound) and draw back a new letter or two.

If it is a true alien word, they can write it under the alien of their choice. If, however, they make a real word, have them identify this (or help them to do so) and 'fine' them one sentence using that word. They love to do this and you'll find a huge number of alien words in one session, while at the same time practising real words successfully.

#alienwords

Magnet poets

'I adore writing poems now.'

This is a brilliant way to take the pressure off creating words when making a poem and allows the children in your group to instantly access poetic opportunities.

There are three ways of making a magnetic poetry set:

- Many ready-made sets are already available online for those short of time (Shakespearean Insults is an adult favourite).
- You can buy magnetic paper sheets that will go through a normal photocopier (check the settings and add it as extra thick card) for you to produce a page of words to use.
- For a really raw poetry experience, simply cut your magnetic paper into strips and write on them with a sharpie and your budding poet, then slice them into words for play.

The aim of this activity is to play around with words and word order. It is fun and inventive, but also reinforces poetic principles, as well as having a lot of words read by the children in your group.

Once made, make sure you have these poems on display – making them on magnetic boards allows you to photocopy them or take pictures with your school tablets.

Teaching tip

Zero budget? Simply blow up a large text, slice into words and use this with the children, sticking their resulting poems onto coloured card.

Taking it further

Blackout poetry uses a similar device, where an extract of text is scoured for keywords in a normal order. These are then circled lightly and the rest of the text 'blacked out' so only the keywords remain.

#magnetpoets

Name it, do it, describe it

'I can now name and sort sentence features quickly and easily.'

Three cut-down milk containers help children no end in identifying the specific features and functions of a sentence, but can be used for a world of other sorting tasks too.

Taking it further

Spray the containers, and colour-code your words to help those children who might need an extra prompt.

Collect (and thoroughly wash) three two-litre milk containers and cut them around the middle so you end up with three tubs. I tend to staple the tubs together too, to avoid 'drift' in the classroom (in other words, to stop me from using them for something else).

Using a whiteboard pen, categorise each bucket with either 'Name', 'Do', 'Describe' or 'Noun', 'Verb', 'Adjective'. Start off by writing down a word that would fit one of these categories and ask the children if it is a naming word, a describing word or a doing word. Leading them to the correct answer, get them to put the word in the correct bucket.

There are so many other ways to use this simple sorting device too:

- Have the children write their own words and then sort them.
- Write a sentence together on a strip of paper, cut it up, then decide where each individual word should go.
- Ask children to sort a collection of words.
- Write down nouns, verbs and adjectives from the story you are about to read or have read with the children, and sort these.
- Fill the containers with about five words each and put a rogue word in each one. Empty the containers one by one and see if the children can identify which word is in the wrong bucket.
- Take one word at random from each bucket and see if you can make a sentence from the three randomly selected words.

#namedodescribe

Word swords

'I can find any word really fast now.'

Enormous fun and hugely educational too – what is not to like about getting children to actively want to look up words in a dictionary or thesaurus?

Arm every child in your group with a dictionary. They stand and put it in an imaginary holster on their side (under their non-dominant arm).

At the command 'draw swords', the children pull out their dictionaries and hold them above their heads. You wait for everyone to be ready, then tell them the word they are searching for.

This is insightful in two ways. Firstly, it gives you as teacher a chance to see the ways children are searching for words in a dictionary (which is often quite painful and awkward if they have not had the practice). Secondly, the competitive edge of the task encourages more concentration.

The child who finds the definition first has to read it aloud. This signals victory for that child but the rest carry on, as victory can be snatched away if they miss out or add a word in the definition. This helps to motivate those lagging to find the word, and the victor to ensure he or she is reading clearly.

After each turn, talk about a specific technique that will help them find the right page. What did they look for? Did they use the keywords at the top and bottom? Did they use their knowledge of the alphabet?

Teaching tip

Ensure where possible that all children in the group use the same dictionary.

Taking it further

This is a great opportunity to target Tier 3 words for a topic – technical vocabulary useful only to that area of study.

#wordswords

Check back

'I found so many more mistakes using the check back.'

Admit it – even checking your own writing as an adult is hard. These three simple strategies can be taught, ideally one-to-one or as a small group, in order to help the children find those errors that would otherwise have gone unnoticed.

Teaching tip

Make two L-shaped cards to help pinpoint individual words and phrases to focus on.

These are the systems I use myself – both on my own in those cold damp nights of report writing and publicly with the class (with the help of my lovely visualiser).

Blind rule check: Use a ruler, turned over, to check each line, one line at a time. The best type of ruler to use with this is opaque, with a slight camber.

Bottom to top: Check spelling by going backwards, bottom to top if you can. We have a natural habit of reading when we check words from left to right, whereas it makes little sense when going in the wrong direction, so we tend to focus more on the words.

Read aloud: Read what you have written aloud – and genuinely aloud, not in your head. Model this for the children whenever possible, but especially in an intervention group, where there is a habit of wanting to 'just get it done and head back'. Checking is an important skill, which can elevate work from 'okay' to 'good' in one quick hit. If there is no one to read aloud to, have them read their work to the tablet. Children love doing this and they spot their mistakes too.

Answer me this: Answer two simple questions when checking any piece of work at the end. Does the work have everything that the reader needs in order to understand what has been written? And if there was one thing you could change to improve the writing, what would it be? Action both answers and repeat.

#checkback

Inspiration station

'I love getting ideas from the inspiration station.'

This small project box is for those children who look at you with blank faces whenever you ask them to write a sentence or paragraph about anything — this is far too broad an opportunity to get something wrong and they end up with creative choke.

Most teachers have an inspiration station of some form or other (they just may not know it, or it might be scattered across their classroom).

You will need a shoebox or equivalent, filled with pictures, quotes, beautiful pieces of writing, snapshots of holidays, blurred photos, unusual objects or trinkets.

At the point at which you see choke flash across children's faces, you know that you can rephrase your question as, 'You can write about anything you like, or the first item I take out of this box. Which would you prefer?' Very often, they will choose the latter.

By choosing a prompt, the pressure is off them to produce something original or noteworthy from the recesses of their mind.

Teaching tip

My current school found this strategy so valuable, they built a room filled with objects to inspire, breed curiosity and excite.

#inspirationstation

Key routes

'I loved plotting a story using the keys.'

Sometimes, you need just one simple prop to help start an imaginative story. Keys are perfect for this.

Find some old keys – the larger and heavier, the better. These can be bought online for a few pounds at popular auction sites. This activity can work well with one child or a small group, but tends to work better with the latter, as they can develop their ideas together.

Start with the key in your hand and explain that you have found it. Explain that to get the key, children have to ask a broad, single-word question, such as 'why?'. Start by holding up the key and ask 'what does this open?'. The child that answers then holds the key and another child can ask the first one-word question. A sample conversation (taken from Year 2) is below:

What does this open?
A secret door.
Where?
In the woods.
Where?
In a big tree.
Why?
A magician is hiding all his stuff there.
Why?
He stole it.
How?
He turned himself invisible...

In the example, you can see how quickly the children come up with suggestions. All the children have been involved in the creation, so they all feel they have a share in it.

#keyroutes

Powerful pottery

'I love seeing my words on display the whole time.'

This quick activity, which can be used as a celebration with your intervention group, takes no time to prepare, but the reward on the children's faces is something to behold.

Go to a local charity shop and find a plain pot or vase, wide enough to fit a roll of sticky labels (the sort your friendly school office might use for address labels). This is your powerful word pot.

Any time a member of your group or class come up with a particularly inspired word, celebrate this by writing this word on a sticky label and sticking it onto the pot. The aim is to cover the pot by a set time – generally a half term is enough to cover a standard pot, although you might be more cautious with some groups.

The pot lives on a windowsill and, once filled, can have a plant or flowers put in it to add some colour to the classroom.

Teaching tip

If you have the time or inclination, you could also do this with Russian dolls, with big words on the larger dolls, and smaller words on the smaller dolls.

#wordpot

Adjective thermometers

'I can find other words which are more impressive to use.'

A simple idea, which reinforces the scale at which a word has impact. These make the use of different words incredibly visual and the children respond well to such a prompt. You'll see other children using them in class too.

Taking it further

Create three thermometers for the current book you are reading, and add the themes of the book above each. Have the children add words for each theme *from* the book on the left, and words they have generated *about* the theme on the right.

Get a copy of the thermometer that is used in Idea 64 and have a selection of thin sticky notes ready for use.

Ask the children, or write for them, all the words you could use to describe temperature. Give them image prompts or descriptions to help them. Put these on separate sticky notes around the thermometer in no particular order.

When the ideas have been exhausted, explain that you'd like them to order the words, from the most cold to the most hot. Demonstrate this on the left hand side of the image of the thermometer and support the children in completing the task.

Review the order they have placed the words in – are there any that need moving around?

Once fully complete, ask them to write down as many words as they can for fear (scared, worried, terrified). Again, when exhausted of ideas, list these on the right-hand side, to see and compare which words are more powerful than others.

This produces a really rich dialogue and debate about the power and impact of words, and is a good strategy for helping some children develop better methods of comparing words.

#adjectivethermometer

Sentence pizzas

'I love using the sentence pizzas to find better words.'

This is the king of gimmicks, yet engages lots of children in using more effective words in their sentences. It can also generate lots of constructive dialogue when you use it.

Divide a circle of card into six sections and draw each of the following separately into the six slices: meat, onions, olives, pineapple, peppers and cheese.

Explain that each of the sections represents a type of word that the children might use, and talk them through the categories:

Meat = a meaty word, one that stands out in its impressiveness, e.g. luminescent

Onions = an eye-watering or emotional word, e.g. broken-hearted

Olives = a disgusting word, e.g. vomit

Pineapple = a word that seems to be out of place from those around it, e.g. football

Peppers = a fairly sensible, healthy word, e.g. nice

Cheese = a word that will make you smile, e.g. chatterbox.

This is a tool to get children to audit the words they and their friends have used in their writing. Have them look through for a meaty word they have used and note it down on the pizza using sticky notes. Do the same for the other categories.

Teaching tip

Have the pizza on display, with the words remaining on it, for other children to add, remove or use.

Taking it further

Ask your local pizza company for a few boxes to make this into an elevated display. A beaming smile and mentioning you are a teacher will work wonders.

#sentencepizzas

Story snakes

'It is so much easier to know where I am with a story now.'

These are deceptively simple story-planning devices and came from work my teacher colleague Clare Stevenson developed in her NQT year (all hail NQTs).

Using your preferred graphics program, design a landscape page with a large backwards S across it. Along the S, place blank circles on its entire length. You have created your first story snake! Print out blanks of these (enlarged onto A3 works best at first).

Use these with a part of a story you are working on, writing down each major event in one of the circles. The children should be able to help you with this.

You can now get the children to do one of several things, all brilliantly versatile:

- Have the children create their own story snake based on the story they have just read.
- Have the children recreate the known story part by part, but allow them one change.
- They can scribe in the circles, or draw a picture to represent each plot event or scene, or even a combination of both.

These work so much more successfully than the traditional 'story mountain', as they don't explicitly show the CONFLICT section of a story, which can often end up in the wrong place on a story mountain. This isn't to say that those story mountain sheets don't have a place, it's just that often the best place is in the recycling.

#storysnakes

Writing temperature

'I know exactly what to do next.'

Often, children can 'choke' in a session on writing because they just don't know what to do next. This uses the idea of cold writing and hot writing, then moves it into a structure that can be followed by all.

With your group and some strips of paper, write down all the stages of writing. These may include:

- ideas
- planning
- word bank
- inspiration
- drafting
- checking
- redrafting
- final copy
- outline
- 'best' handwriting
- submission.

Search online for a blank thermometer image, and print it out in colour as large as your printer will allow. Laminate it for long lasting benefit. Ask the children to place the stages correctly on the thermometer, in the right order. As you do this, discuss the different aspects involved in each stage. Some children might benefit from equipment prompts or pictures.

This activity helps to identify the areas of writing that the children are most and least secure in, and also helps to guide a child to the next stage of the writing process, to avoid the 'I don't know what to do next' statements.

Teaching tip

This makes a quick working wall display. You can put a neon arrow where the children should be, add the days of the week to show expected progress, or even pin examples of work at the different stages in order to help children through modelling.

#writingtemp

Word maps

'The ideas just kept coming with word prompts.'

Which child doesn't love a map or maze? This activity combines this love with a passion for vocabulary, which will become apparent after using this brilliant inspiration tool.

With a large piece of paper and some felt pens or a magic whiteboard (see Idea 94), ask each of the children in your group to make a small circular mark towards the left of the paper. They should then take their pen on a leisurely journey across the page, intersecting itself, and make a destination mark. Giving each child a different coloured pen makes this instantly more appealing.

Next, ask the children to decide a genre for their line. This could be: historical, comedy, school, animal, sports, family, horror or fantasy. They should write this genre at the start and end of their line.

Next, they go along their own line and write a word or phrase that they might find in their chosen genre where lines intersect. The children will take to this quickly after a few examples and can help each other out. The task also helps to define what a specific genre might, or might not, feature.

A-ppealing emotions

'I always remember this lesson.'

This lesson will stop your SLT dead in their tracks if they come across you and a child, both crying, with onions in front of you. Behind the high gimmick factor of this lesson is the stickability of the intervention, which simply does not go away.

With the group, gather a chopping board and an onion, and a large sheet of paper to write down new phrases.

Explain that you are going to scribe for the children the phrases you might feel for a character at a sad point in their writing. Explain that you can only accept a phrase from someone who has just peeled a layer of the onion and that the new phrase has to be more emotive than the previous one.

Begin by demonstrating to the children a very mild sad phrase after you've taken a layer off, and start passing the onion around the room.

This may alert the gimmick klaxon, but it works to concentrate the minds (and tear ducts) of the children and creates a very visceral prompt in their memories for building on emotion.

Teaching tip

Have children wash their hands after the task. The recommended time to wash is the length of time it takes to sing *Happy Birthday*, twice. Try it – it really works!

#onionfeelings

First class words

'Everyone wants to have their word delivered.'

If you have an orange juice carton, a little time and a passable Elvis Presley singing voice, this little task is one that will grow and grow until the whole class will want in. Take time with the preparation — it's worth it.

Make the ultimate sacrifice and buy a large carton of juice — the bigger, the better. Enjoy the drink! Next, cover or spray-paint the carton red, adding a black top if you have the time/resources/patience. Cut a postbox-style slot in the front and make a large opening hatch in the back.

This is a postbox for first class words — words that strike you as being impressive, powerful or relevant. Demonstrate how to use it by highlighting words you have spotted, writing these words on a slip of paper and having the child who wrote them post them in your postbox. Choose a terribly boring word (e.g. nice, good, said) from your own work and ask whether it should go in the postbox. The group should answer with a resounding 'NO!'. This is when you all sing the classic *Return to Sender*. (You dress up as a witch on World Book Day, so get over your pride!)

Draw a line through the boring word and take suggestions for improvement. Once a successful word has been chosen, write it on the back and choose someone to post that word.

#firstclasswords

Vocab tracker

'I am learning so many new words now.'

Growing children's vocabulary has to be a priority for all teachers and this activity gives a prescribed structure to developing new vocabulary, with definite understanding as the end goal.

Begin by preparing a writing frame with the following along the top of a landscape A4 piece of paper:

- Vocabulary
- I have never seen this word
- I don't know this word
- I think I know this word
- I definitely know this word.

Allow for 12 rows below these column headings.

Add the 12 words you would like to teach the children in your group along the left side of the sheet. You may want to teach these three at a time, but the task itself will help you.

Ask the children if they have heard or know the words in the list one by one. They should tick the appropriate box alongside that word. Knowing a word means both understanding what it means and being able to put it in a sentence correctly.

With this complete, you have a reasonably accurate baseline on which to build vocabulary with the children. Introduce each word to the children over successive weeks (at a practical pace), starting with those words they haven't even heard. Talk about the word, what it looks like, what it means (don't just use the dictionary definition) and some ways you could use it. Have them repeat these words back to you. After each session, go through the list again and log any movement.

#vocabtracker

Stick insect blog

'Brad is the best pet ever.'

Nothing beats a stimulus for exciting the children's interest, and for next to nothing, you can have your very own class pet do this for you.

Teaching tip

The reward for best entry can hold the stick insect on their hand – enormous fun!

Stick insects are easily obtainable from pet shops, or willingly given away by hobby breeders – you may even have someone at school with stick insects. They live on privet and sprayed stale water, so there is no cost here either. Lastly, you will need a small fish tank or similar, with a closed but porous lid.

With your group, name your stick insect, and invent a ludicrous backstory for him or her. Our stick insect, Brad, was a top athlete who was turned into a very sleepy stick insect after being caught cheating in a running race.

Create a blog or diary for your stick insect and model a starting entry. This can be as simple as a single sentence, or a more detailed paragraph. It could be his inner frustration at being trapped in a stick insect's body, or her love of privet.

Taking it further

Try having a child read to your pet – oddly enough, the children respond really well to this.

#stickinsectblog

Keep up the blog or diary-writing as a fantastic starting activity for your group each time you meet. It only takes a few minutes and is so rewarding for the children to read previous entries.

Sloth weekend diary

'A welcome respite to action-packed weekend diaries.'

Parents will be familiar with the weekend class mascot diary, where parents can end up competing to have the most adventurous or action-packed weekend ever. This offers a completely different experience, usually with hilarious diary entries as a result.

Slothy the sloth was a stuffed toy chosen by the class as their take-home toy. Instead of asking the children to write about their high-octane weekend with Slothy, they are asked to have a calm and relaxing weekend. This is a fantastic idea for a class or group to carry out because it takes the focus away from actual reporting to a much more fun creative-writing task.

It is best started with a model page from the teacher. A morning latte in the coffee shop, lie-ins and popcorn movie night with Slothy (or your chosen toy) all make for entertaining reading and photographs. The parents will immediately understand what the project is about and enter into the spirit when it is their turn.

Teaching tip

Ask the children to read their entries in character on Monday, for added entertainment.

#slothdiary

Handwriting and presentation skills

Part 8

Benchmarks

'Whenever my handwriting slides, I always check my benchmark.'

Ask a primary teacher about their frustrations with secondary education and one thing they will say is the decline in children's handwriting when they move up, even after seven years of focus on cursive script. This idea solves this problem in the present, in just one task.

Find a simple poem to copy, and prepare your workspace for optimum handwriting – plain paper with line guides and paper clips, good lighting, and clean surfaces.

Explain to your group that they will be writing out the simple poem on the page provided. The only rule is that it must be the neatest work that they have ever produced.

Help the children with their handwriting, giving them every support. After completing their work, trim the poem and then stick it down on the inside front of their writing book cover. Any time their writing diminishes, ask them to check their handwriting benchmark. They have inadvertently demonstrated just what is possible.

#benchmarks

Get a grip

'My handwriting is so much better.'

As a southpaw with handwriting more suited to a doctor than a teacher, I have every sympathy with the challenges that some children face with handwriting. These tips for improving grip will help your children no end.

Pick and flick
This works best with pencils taken from an upright container, nibs pointing up. Using the thumb and first finger, pinch a pencil around a quarter of the way down the stem. Pull it out of the pot, then flip it backward so it rests on the V space between your finger and thumb joint. This simple action can be transformative for some children who get in a real muddle with how to hold a pencil correctly.

Lines
Use lines for the children that are just slightly smaller than you would like them to write. Put a dot where you would like them to start. Encourage the children to write on every other line until their descenders are fluid.

Odd pairings
Have the children practise the odd pairings that join at the top, rather than starting again at the bottom. 'r+' is a prime example; if children have been trained to start every letter from the bottom, joining an r to an a makes 'na' not 'ra'.

Pencil grips
Some teachers love these for training the children to use the correct finger hold, while others recognise that they only work for one type of pencil and not the host of other writing tools the children use. I would advise using them judiciously and removing them as quickly as possible. Treat them like stabilisers – they are a tool to help write, not a permanent fixture.

Teaching tip

If the children start every line a little further along each time, ending up with a wedge of blank space, the sticker of a bus (from my repeated comment 'you could park a bus in that space') works a treat in curbing this.

#getagrip

Left behind

'Making my working space left-friendly has made such a difference to my handwriting.'

Although 10% of your class are likely to be left-handed, this often goes unnoticed in the classroom. These small changes can lead to enormous gains for those pupils.

Teaching tip

Whenever you change your seating plan, check afterwards that left-handers are on the left on a double desk.

These strategies all helped me and may help anyone else in your class who is a left-hander.

Desk positioning

This is the most significant change you can make for the children who are left-handed in your class. Ensure that if you use double desks, the left-handers in your class are sitting on the left-hand side. To see the problem this can cause if you don't do this, swap them over and watch elbow wars occur!

Book positioning

Any teachers who stick words, work or tasks into the books and keep them to the margin might want to observe how a left-handed child copes. For a right-hander, their work leads away from the task sheets, whereas for the leftie, their work leads over. This is a small but significant feature for them. If you are using structure strips, stick them on the right-hand side of a page to help the lefties out.

Handwriting

Similarly, a little sympathy is needed for their writing position. Again, a left-handed person is always covering up what they are handwriting, whereas a right-hander is revealing theirs. To manage this, lefties often do the strangest things with book positioning – sometimes they end up at the oddest angles. Try where possible to let them have as much space as they need; they can find it hard to manage a more conventional writing book or textbook layout.

Taking it further

Mark an 'L' on the back of writing books, as this will remind you of the challenges left-handers can face.

#leftbehind

It's a snip

'Cutting out has never been more effective.'

As soon as you start cutting out for the children, they stop learning how to control the cut. These activities help to refine the gross and fine motor skills of scissor action in your group or class.

These strategies all need a little preparation, but really help to master scissor skills with the children. Developing these skills is much more effective when done as part of a small group.

Cs and Ss

Draw some large capital Cs and Ss around the edge of an A4 sheet of paper which has been cut in half lengthways. Demonstrate to the children that these letters can be cut out with one long and careful cut, rather than little snipping cuts, and demonstrate how to put the base of the blade against the line, then cut by moving the paper rather than scissors when possible.

Patterns

The next stage is to put a variety of handwriting patterns in a tray with some scissors. Use lines, curves, waves and zigzags. Tell the children they can choose to cut these out during any free time, but they need to use as few cuts as possible. Children count how many cuts each makes and write their name and this number at the end. They will love having a 'Top of the Cuts' chart, showing the names and scores of the best cutters.

Jigsaw cutting

The final strategy develops accuracy. Children take a pen on a wander around a page of A4, doodling slowly over the page, crossing lines and not taking their pen off the page until the end. They then cut this out, following the line as carefully as possible. When all cut out, put it together as if it were a jigsaw.

Teaching tip

Avoid left-handed scissors where possible. The blade is the opposite side but, in practice, I've only ever found one child who could use them effectively.

#itsasnip

Who rules?

'My lines are now straight every time.'

It may seem indulgent to spend time practising drawing straight lines but it has huge benefits for your class. If you have ever sighed at the mess some ruler work leaves, you will love these strategies.

We ask children to use their rulers all the time, but do they actually know how to use them? These quick skills-recaps, when taught in small groups by the teacher or TA, really help to reset their understanding and the versatility of the humble ruler. But first, some requests.

Choose a 30cm white ruler, with cm one side and mm on the other, and a double camber (angled edges). This may seem very specific, but all the variations cause problems:

- 15cm just isn't long enough
- inches on rulers are confusing
- clear rulers are a pain and can't be used for tracking skills
- fold-up rulers are convenient but inaccurate, and you always end up with a dip at 15cm.

Holding a ruler in place
The children love this. Write a series of words over a sheet of paper, with a variety of angles, and show how to underline each word:

Position the ruler clearly underneath the word.

Using the non-writing hand, spread the fingers out along the top of the ruler (this is 'spider fingers') and push DOWN (not up).

Draw the pencil across the ruler space, not against the ruler. The aim is to draw a line, not to fight with the ruler.

Measuring accurately

Have a page with a series of lines in all shades, thicknesses and angles. Demonstrate how to measure using the ruler accurately. Look at the size of the line – is it better to use the cm side or mm side? Place the 0 at the very end of the line. Ensure the ruler follows the line accurately. Using a pencil, show how you are using it to point to the end of the line and draw it down so that it points to the exact measurement.

Felt pen flipping

Some adults may not know about this technique, despite being in front of a ruler all their lives. If you are using felt pens to make a line, use this technique for a smudge-free mark:

- Turn the ruler over.
- Position the ruler in place and then tilt it forward, so the lip of the ruler is touching the paper.
- Hold the ruler in place by pushing down on the downturned camber.
- Draw the line by drawing across, not against.
- When the line has been drawn, relax the ruler so that it folds back and away from the page. No smudging!

Bonus idea ★

Keep a line of rulers attached to the bottom of your whiteboard so that they are always available, visually and physically.

#whorules

Chopstick challenges

'I'm not sure I was learning as it was so much fun.'

The humble pair of chopsticks is a great way of aiding gross and fine motor skills — but this task will take great perseverance.

Teaching tip

Chopsticks sets can be bought from pound shops on the high street, or from popular online auction sites, and last for ages. Alternatively, charm the local restaurant into helping you out!

Chopsticks are a great skill-builder, which will help the children to manipulate any tool in their hands. Try these techniques with any age from Reception upwards.

Holding the sticks
Begin by learning how to hold a pair of chopsticks. Any number of YouTube clips can help you with this, but the principle is always the same — the bottom stick rests in the finger/thumb valley and remains static, while the top stick is adjusted to move up and down. The wrist carries out a lot of pivoting, so start with the simpler tasks.

Hook a hoop
Place a series of Hula Hoops® or similar on the table so their hoop is visible both sides (standing up). The children use one stick to collect them, then pour them into a pot.

Extend this by having some hoops flat and some standing up. What do they have to do with just the chopsticks to collect the hoops?

Transfer
Have two cups, one filled with holed beads or Multilink® cubes. Simply transfer these to the other pot using only the chopsticks. What is the best technique and why?

Buried treasure
This is a variant on the task above. Have a few cups, with a range of objects hidden just below a layer of flour. The flour adds a new challenge to the task.

Bonus idea ★

Jelly fishing
This is the ultimate challenge. Buy a packet of jelly cubes or similar, cut them up and put them in a cup. Again, the challenge is to transfer these to another cup. Gamify this by using a timer — what is the fastest a child can transfer them?

#chopstickchallenge

Social skills – friendships, teamwork and managing emotions

Part 9

Friendship rings

'I get now why I can't work with everyone the whole time.'

Ah, the complex minefield that is friendships. Avoid telling the children that it's even more complex as an adult and instead use friendship rings to help the children establish how they operate with their friends.

This activity is the perfect conflict resolution activity, which helps children on the odd day in which they find it hard to identify exactly how friendships work.

Create a simple template of a circle with three or four outer rings and copy enough for everyone in your group, plus one for the adult (I have a batch of these on standby).

Explain that all their friends are on this page but some are closer to you than others. Ask them to write their name or draw themselves in the middle. On the next ring out, ask them to write in up to five names of the children they are closest to. Talk to them about how they have chosen them and why.

Fill up the rings, working outward in both closeness and distance. Now choose one person from the innermost ring and ask about a time that they have fallen out. Where would they be put then?

Explain that friendship is ever-changing and ever-moving, and although they have written the names down here now, this might change. It doesn't matter that friendships change; they are still at the centre and they control who they are closest to on that page.

Group work rules

'I don't feel like I'm doing all the work now.'

Understanding group dynamics is key to helping a group work together. These five simple steps make all the difference and are best taught explicitly.

How can children know how to work as a group and really learn together, if they haven't been trained? Enter SCORE, a handy acronym to help you define the rules for working as a group.

Share ideas

Compliment others

Offer help or encouragement

Recommend changes kindly

Exercise self control.

You will need to teach each of these skills explicitly. Have the SCORE rules written or typed and visible in the classroom. Go through each principle in turn, modelling good and bad examples.

Next, simulate a discussion (e.g. 'Invent a robot to clear up litter at school') and, during this discussion, highlight the positive ways the SCORE system is operating.

Teaching tip

Share the SCORE system in a staff meeting. If you are brave enough, role-play praise when someone demonstrates one of the core skills you have spoken about.

#groupworkrules

Country collage

'I have learnt so much about France.'

This activity involves teamwork, research and a little artistic flair, but the results are stunning.

Find online an outline of a country – France is a really good first choice. Print this out and enlarge it with your photocopier until it covers the space of several A3 sheets of paper.

Join these together with masking tape and have a selection of tablets, pictures and holiday brochures available.

Explain that you are going to make a country collage with your group about the country in question. Start by brainstorming what comes to mind when they think of that country and start building up a bank of words to look up.

Begin collecting images and have the children research different aspects of the pictures too. If you chose wine, where are the wine regions of France? Stick the vineyard pictures in that region on your picture.

The aim should be a word-free collage of a country, with the children in your group confident enough to speak about the different pictures and explain the features and aspects of that country. It works fantastically well as an intervention because, in a class-run activity of this type, misconceptions can quickly creep into the finished work. By keeping the work to a small group, you can give immediate feedback and guidance.

#countrycollage

Echo skills

'It was like Chinese whispers, but with craft.'

Using this activity demonstrates very clearly both the need to follow instructions from others carefully and how we can learn from each other.

In a circle, give each child a square of origami paper (or A4 paper cut into a square). Explain that you will make an origami shape together, but there are two clear rules:

1. There is to be no speaking.
2. You can only do what the person on the left does.

Now make an origami model (you'll need to make one beforehand a few times so that you feel confident enough to lead the activity).

Take your time, ensuring that each stage is perfectly replicated by the person on your left, their left, and so on. This may seem bizarre, but it actually works more effectively than you carrying out a stage of folding, and then everyone repeating it at the same time. Encourage silence and careful visual following instead.

At the end, you should end up with the same shape (with an acceptable variance in quality). What did everyone learn from the process? Ask them to explain this as fully as possible.

Teaching tip

The classic 'chatterbox' origami model is a perfect starting model to make. Search online for the best way to make this.

#echoskills

Face fits

'I can identify lots of emotions now.'

This activity requires a little preparation, but will bring a whole new dimension to the children's visual literacy, as well as linking to other topics with ease.

Collect together several series of photographs. Your base set should be a series of faces showing a range of emotions. These are easily found online, or use CC Search (Creative Commons) to help you find images with lighter copyright restrictions.

Collect another set of images that could relate to feelings. Weather types are perfect for this, e.g. a stormy night, a sunny day, rain on a window.

When talking to the children, either individually or as a small group, you can do one of several activities:

- Match the emotion to the weather type.
- Describe the weather type as an emotion.
- Rate the emotions from happy to sad.

The key with all the activities is the dialogue that is generated by the discussions. This is often very rich and enabling for children who struggle to explain how they are feeling.

Pompom conversation

'I loved making this craft and it was fun to talk too.'

This activity combines a very simple craft with some effective strategies to talk about feelings or worries with a small group of children. The resulting pompom ends up as a symbolic reminder of what has been covered too.

Prepare two bagel-shaped sections of cardboard and gather together a collection of wool – enough for each member of the group.

In the example below, I am using the concept of feelings of frustration to explain how you could run a session, but you could use this idea with a range of emotions.

Feelings of frustration

Give an example of a time when you have felt frustrated. Can the children think of times when they have felt frustrated? Talk about these, wrapping wool around the bagels for each of the feelings mentioned. As you do so, talk to the children about how they might address these feelings. This could be through:

- Acknowledging the feelings.
- Sharing their frustrations with others.
- Taking clear action to counter the feelings.

For each solution, wrap more wool around the bagels. As you do this, help the children to predict when they are most likely to feel these frustrations and what they can do to counter getting into these situations.

The end of the session is the best part! Symbolically cut around the outside of the bagel templates, in between them ideally, then tie a length of wool between the inside of the two pieces, joining all the 'strategies' up. This can then be used as a physical reminder to the children next time they feel frustrated.

Teaching tip

This is a lovely activity to do with a nurture group.

#pompoms

Thought park

'I love finding out what ride I'm on.'

This is an ongoing intervention for children who find it hard to explain their feelings, which can often affect how they feel in the classroom itself.

Go to the website of your local theme park and download the map, or search online for a child-friendly one with pictures of the rides.

Show the map to the children and talk about the rollercoaster of a day you've had so far (got locked out, found a treat in your pigeon hole, forgot to mark last night's books). Some creative licence may be necessary (but in all honesty probably isn't needed!). Explain that if your day was a ride on that map, you feel that it would be most like the rollercoaster, because of all the twists and turns, highs and lows that you've had so far.

Have the children study the map and explain to you and the others exactly how they are like one of the rides, and why. The explanation is the key point here – this activity should help to unpick exactly how they are feeling, if not how they got there at the start.

Finally, explain that although sometimes they *have* to go on certain rides, there is a lot of level time in between – life isn't all highs and lows.

#thoughtpark

Fizzy can angry

'I know how to calm down now.'

One simple prop can help alleviate the stress that some children can feel and this distraction strategy has worked wonders for a whole range of children.

This was used to help one child who would have sudden outbursts, but be unable to pinpoint exactly why they had exploded in such a fashion after something so seemingly trivial.

With a can of carbonated drink, ask the child what would happen if you opened the can. They should be able to explain that the can would fizz a little and be pourable straight away. Now explain that you might have had a bad journey into work (shake the can a little), that you slipped over in the toilets (shake), got jostled on the stairs up (shake a little more), dropped your bag (quick vigorous shake), and then had a maths lesson that made you nervous because it was a new topic to teach (put the can on your nervous, shaking leg).

Ask the child what might happen if you opened the can now. They should be able to explain that it would fizz up everywhere. Highlight that it looks no different from the outside. Is that how they feel sometimes?

Develop a way for the child to indicate when their can has been shaken up and explain that it is okay to feel shaken, but that they mustn't open the can until the contents have settled. At the end of the day, open the can with them, showing that the can has settled once more.

Teaching tip

A fizzy drink bottle can be more visual for some children (and is less dangerous if in the wrong hands!).

#fizzycanangry

101

Inhabiting a character

'I just like speaking as someone else.'

Even the most reticent child can start contributing using an indirect speaking tool. Here are some ideas to get you started.

Wooden spoons

Print out pictures of some simple characters and tack them onto wooden spoons. As simple as this is, having a child in your group have the spoon character speak really can make a sizeable difference for some children. Likewise, having them hold up the spoon character who is speaking can help them discern characters in a story more effectively.

Masks

These are not used enough in schools. Masks seem to provide an incredible platform for some children to speak without the pressure of it being on them personally. Neutral face masks are available and can be quickly decorated as necessary.

Puppets

Again, these are gold beyond the Reception class and can be used in any class, especially with the right teacher. Children can respond to a puppet in a different way, can read to them without judgement, and love having a puppet read their work back.

Jaw talk

Take a face-on photograph of a character, actor or animal, copy this twice, and fold one photo at mouthline, folding the lower mouth behind. Do the reverse on the other photo and attach a lollipop stick to the lower section. You have a (primitive, admittedly) talking mouth. This is great for practising direct speech work in which a character is saying something.

Ready to learn – behaviour, motivation and memory

Part 10

Pupil manifesto

'This was our very own creation.'

Parents new to a school often get a prospectus, but what about the children who are going? Making a pupil manifesto is a great way for a child to reflect on what actually happens for them at school.

The pupil manifesto idea came from a child joining a school with severe autism spectrum disorder and the parents had been advised to make a book helping to introduce him to the school. What a fantastic idea for all new children!

Share with the group your school prospectus and explain who it is for. Tell them you'd like to make one for new children rather than new parents and start taking ideas for what should be included. Be warned – the children will not be backward in coming forward at this point!

Start by making a scrapbook of ideas. Write a title on each page of the sorts of things to cover and think about what images and text you'd want on each page.

You might want to work on this a page at a time, or ask different children to work on different pages. However it is set up, support the children in their ideas, presentation and vocabulary. Reinforce that this is a book to be shared between parents and children.

The children will love making this book together and will have a finished product at the end. It will showcase their writing and design skills too.

Pomodoro targets

'I can work for far longer than I thought now.'

The Pomodoro Technique of timing yourself to be wholeheartedly productive for 25 minutes can also have the same impact on the children in your class. Although ticking timers are best, simply searching for 'x minutes timer' in your browser will support this too.

Using a kitchen timer has worked wonders for my own personal focus strategies and it can help the children too.

Begin by giving the child you are working with a timer and show them that you are setting it to three minutes. Explain that they have to work as hard as they can for all the time that it is ticking, until the bell goes off.

The ticking is both a motivator and a pressure device, and while it doesn't suit some children, it can be incredibly motivating for others.

When they have completed three minutes and the timer goes off, celebrate this and record the time. Extend this to four minutes and begin again.

Keep extending it, bearing in mind that a child's concentration span is their age plus a minute (making my concentration span 32 minutes). Celebrate every ring, highlighting just how much can be achieved with applied concentration.

Ensure the amount of work you give is just over what would be possible for that child in the given time.

Teaching tip

This technique was named after the pomodoro tomato, once a popular timer shape. The popular Swedish hotdog store IKEA® also sells furniture and kitchen equipment – who knew? Their ticking timers are inexpensive and perfect for this activity.

#pomodoro

Fidget tips

'I get far less distracted in class.'

Low-level fiddling by some children can end up as high-level frustration for some teachers. These short and quick fixes can, with a little training, cure lots of the issues.

This works as an in-class intervention and involves nothing more complex than a loop of wool, around 30cm long, tied on the framework of the child's chair. Sorry, fidget spinners, you are just too annoying.

Explain to the child that they have been given a fiddle loop and that you have discovered that playing with a loop has been shown to increase concentration (and I'd love someone to actually research this properly!).

Tie the wool (around 30cm is perfect) and triple knot it to the joining bar of the chair. This will allow the child to access it easily while, at the same time, not proving a distraction.

The children are endlessly inventive with the way they play with the woollen loop and will be more focused when you are teaching them.

Is this an intervention? I believe so. It intervenes with those children who experience choke when learning and gives them a way of distracting themselves from the anxiety they can feel, especially when in a small group (and thus under more pressure to perform).

Framing tasks

'I love focusing on one thing using the frames.'

The use of frames helps children to focus on just one area of their work, which can make the pressure of improving everything far less arduous. Although this works best with writing improvements, it can also be used for maths too.

Find some cartoon picture frames of all shapes and sizes on a search engine's image libraries, and print them out in colour. Cut them out so that they are hollow inside (like a picture frame), then laminate them. Don't cut out the laminate on the inside of the frame.

With these frames in front of the children, tell them that they will use a frame to focus in on just one part of their work. Let them decide which frame to use and place it over a part of their work (you could tack it in place to avoid slippage).

Go through the work in the frame, adding punctuation, correcting spellings, even changing words. Make the corrections on the frame itself using board pens.

When complete, take away the frame and ask the children to make the corrections in their actual work.

Teaching tip

Note down the frame children used each session and remove it from their options in the next session. This stops the clever child who chooses the smallest frame each time.

Taking it further

These frames work just as well in a whole-class situation for focused writing correction.

#frameme

Remote control

'I love the instructions remote control.'

A little preparation is involved here, but gives a good alternative to using verbal cues with children and really helps to prompt the group you are working with to focus.

Create a simple remote control template and ensure it has the following:

- numbers 1–9 (for the steps needed)
- play button (for how to know when to start)
- rewind button (what to do when it goes wrong)
- fast forward button (how you know when it is finished)
- pause button (reasons to leave the activity).

You may come up with other necessary buttons, e.g. a menu guide for equipment lists and so on.

Talk through the remote control and say it is the guide to help children complete a task clearly. Talk through the stages of the task and write each stage as simply as possible on the board. The most effective instructions lead with a verb. Number the stages 1–9 and 'press' the button as you reach each stage.

#remotecontrol

Talk through the rest of the buttons and have this remote on display throughout the task.

Managing the reluctant attendee

'I like going out now.'

Things have changed more dramatically than you might at first think. Ten years ago, the school I worked in had a special needs department situated in the basement – you literally went 'downstairs'. Despite the changes, some children are still reluctant to attend interventions. These tips will help you motivate them.

Top and tail work

Turn a scrapbook 90 degrees sideways, so that children are greeted with two A4 landscape pages. Add workings (word lists, assistant notes, spelling attempts, etc.) to the top half and their final work to the bottom half. This can motivate the most reluctant attendee, as well as enabling you to plot their progress.

Straw rewards

This takes a little set-up. Pin a strong plastic straw horizontally to the wall with a map pin. Staple a money bag to each end and put some sort of reward in one bag. Have this very visually available to the child. Whenever they attend their intervention, add a small item to the other bag. If gravity doesn't help move the straw, give it some assistance! Once the straw is vertical, the child may have the reward. This is a slow burner, but is also enormously rewarding.

Ask me about. . . stickers

Although you might already be using stickers for your intervention students, the others in your class will soon want one. Create a set of bespoke stickers with the words 'Ask me about. . . ' on them followed by what you have covered. Prime the rest of your staff to stop and ask about whatever is on the sticker. It is astounding the impact that this can have on a young child's confidence.

#reluctantlearners

Memory palace

'I can remember so much better now.'

This is a very old technique, used for hundreds of years; with small groups, this technique will not only help them to remember a list of items, but will also empower them by challenging their self-perception.

Teaching tip

To get the best out of this activity, use it almost immediately afterwards to help them learn then recall an actually beneficial list – the rules for starting a new paragraph, for example.

Memory palaces are used the world over to help people remember non-linked items. Start by finding ten items from a recently-studied book and place them in ten distinct places around your school. Although you can get away with using large images, finding actual items works best.

Take the children in your group on a tour of the school in a circular route, stopping and highlighting each item as you come across it. Emphasise to the group the actual features of the object and the location it has been placed at in the school.

Returning to the work space, talk the children through the school again, prompting them to recall the different items they found on their journey. You will be surprised by their impressive recall!

Explain how they can use this technique for learning lists of items or strategies that they can use in class. Highlight that they are memory masters now!

#memorypalace

Bun shoe tree

'I can remember items in a list really easily now.'

I have used bun shoe tree for many years now, as it elicits a genuine level of joy from even the shyest of children. It is totally engaging and encourages great creative play too.

Before you begin, you'll have to do a little learning yourself. Learn the following rhyming pairs:

one=bun; two=shoe; three=tree; four=door; five=hive; six=sticks; seven=heaven; eight=gate; nine=vine; ten=pen.

With the group, make a shopping list of items you need to get this weekend. Have them make up items for the list; it will prove you aren't cheating. Put these in a numbered list from one to ten.

Look at the first item and create a really outrageous image that connects the item to a bun. Explain that one rhymes with bun. If the item was a bike for example, tell the story of a man who goes to eat a bun and bites into it, only to discover that it is filled with a bike. The more quirky and original the idea, the better – these are the images that stick in the child's mind.

Complete the list, then hide it from them. Ask children to think of their own visual image for each item and the linked rhyming word.

Ask them what one was and prompt them to solve this by remembering what one stood for (bun) and how this was connected to the list (bike). Do this for all the numbers, then pull out the best challenge: 'Who thinks they can talk through the entire list?'

Help them where needed and get to this point with each child. You can extend this by asking them, 'what was three?' or 'what number was the newspaper?'. You'll all be amazed at their ability to solve the problems so quickly!

Teaching tip

Learning this skill is a dream for children who struggle to remember items or lists, as they come up with imaginative ideas to use.

Taking it further

Work with the children to see if they can come up with rhyming words for the numbers 11 to 20.

#bunshoetree

Resources for interventions

Part 11

My tech dream team

'I love my tech, but these three tools are transformative.'

These are three tech tools I would take on my teaching desert island. The island would have to have mains electricity, and I'm not sure I'd be teaching, but the image is secure in your head.

Magic whiteboard
This is a statically-charged white plastic sheet, roughly A2 in size, that sticks to practically anything. It has even been used by diminutive teachers in classrooms where the whiteboard was placed too high. It makes big teaching spaces ideal in any location and wipes clean so you won't have to replace it very often. Worth its weight in gold and perfect for those portable intervention sessions that sometimes occur.

Visualiser
These simple 'cameras on sticks' have been around a while, but they are only just coming into their own in terms of proper use. They are fantastic for modelling and even more effective for the redrafting stage of writing, with one piece of volunteer work under the camera. For intervention work, the visualiser is amazing for celebrating great work on the big screen.

Label printer
Many teachers don't even know the label printer exists, yet they can transform many aspects of your classroom organisation. About the size of a small shoe box, the printer is fitted with a roll of thermal paper and connects to your computer. Using the accompanying software, you can make labels of virtually any size or shape, and print off one or lots. They even slice the labels for you. The resultant labels can be used for feedback, job titles, visitor badges, registers for trips, guided reading groups – the options really are only limited by your imagination.

#teachertech

Magnetic letters

'I really know my letters well now.'

Inexpensive and ubiquitous, magnetic letters still aren't used as much as they could be in interventions, especially in junior class interventions. Here are some strategies to reverse this trend.

Postbox letters

Using a home-made postbox (see Idea 67 for how to make one), collect sets of letters the child is confused with. Have them draw the letters off the table one by one and post them in, sounding out the letter each time.

Root words

Write a root word in the centre of the magnetic board and have collections of magnetic letters that can be used to make prefixes and suffixes. Ask the child to expand the root word using the letters provided. Back this up by having them record their answers.

Fill in the blank

Using the magnetic letters, write out several words with missing letters. Give the child a collection of magnetic letters and ask them to select which letter correctly fills each blank. This activity is especially good for words with silent letters (knife or sword, for example) and popular misspellings.

Initial sound match

Have a range of pictures available (laminated because you work in primary), with a pot of magnetic letters that correspond to the first letter of the objects depicted. Ask the children to pair up the pictures and letters. This activity is perfect for those who can't hear that initial letter.

> **Teaching tip**
>
> Although the temptation is to buy the cheapest set of magnetic letters, examine them carefully, as some sets have very unusual or vague formations, which will confuse some children.

> **Bonus idea**
>
> **Quicksand**
>
> This activity is ADORED by juniors, who rarely get to use the fun equipment by that age. Display a selection of keywords and hide from view a set of pots containing magnetic letters that make up these words. Take one pot and bury the letters in a shallow container filled with play sand. The child pulls out one letter at a time and tries to work out which word is buried before all the letters are unearthed. Warning: children get enormously competitive – even with themselves!

#magneticletters

Dear diary

'It was my favourite book to take home.'

The appeal of a new, personal book cannot be underestimated in the primary classroom. For very little expense, making a diary book for all sorts of purposes ticks this box and many more besides.

Teaching tip

There is no reason why you couldn't keep one of these for yourself too.

Just after new year, retailers heavily discount their diary books. These are perfect for using with an intervention child. Here are just a few of the many ways they can be utilised:

Feelings book
Have the child record their feelings every day. This could be through words, pictures, drawings or even cut-outs. This can be public (working with an adult) or private (which some children respond to well).

Just one sentence
Ask the child to write just one sentence every day. After they have written it, add a target for the next day. This could be to use a comma, add two adjectives or describe an object. There are a wealth of 'creativity muse' books on the market – plunder them for inspiration.

Short-form reflection book
For the more creative, writing a short-form poem at the end of each day is a great way to get a snapshot of life. These are barely a few words, so take little to no time, yet position a feeling in words, which some children respond to very successfully.

Gratitude book
Writing down three things a child was pleased with, took delight in, or was grateful for, can be incredibly therapeutic. The real bonus with this idea is the reward that comes when previous entries are read back.

#deardiary

A4 offcuts

'I love using these little slips of paper.'

The bane of many a teacher are the many strips of paper that pile up near guillotines. Don't throw them away; instead, utilise them in lessons. Here are some ideas for how they can be used in class.

Achievements paper chain
Children write an achievement they have made on a strip at the end of the week. Link these up to make a small paper chain and hang it up. Imagine the length of chain you would have if you did this every week for a year!

Word reveal
Write some words clearly on a length of paper. Hide the paper under some card and slowly pull out the paper, revealing the words one letter at a time. Children score a point every time they identify the word correctly.

Bookmarks
Use the strips as bookmarks, with the children writing down words they like on the paper as they go. When the strip is complete, stick it in the inside front cover of their writing book for word inspiration.

Sentence models
Have a stack of these ready. Choose a sentence the child has written or co-constructed and write it on a strip. Cut up the sentence with the children, reading the words as you cut them up. Mix up the words and have the child reconstruct the sentence. Keep the full stop separate to secure their understanding.

Teaching tip

Never throw these away; instead, use an old copier paper lid to store them. Children love using the strips for all sorts of imaginative work.

#A4offcuts

Support mats

'Whenever I get stuck, I can turn to my mat.'

Search for any subject and 'mats' in a search engine, and you'll be greeted with a whole profusion of options to print out and laminate. Don't underestimate the ways these can be used in your sessions.

A good support mat used well can be the backbone of your intervention sessions.

Try where possible to have these printed out in colour on A3 paper and laminate them into reusable states as quickly as you can. Here are some ways you can use them:

Work mats
Use them as place settings for the children. They will know where to sit and know where they can go for help when wrong too. Try where possible to have children 'find help' rather than pointing it out for them, to encourage their independence.

Reference mats
These are mats placed above (away from) where the child works and referred to when the child gets stuck. These are particularly valuable when used for sound groups, table facts or visual examples of a topic, such as groups of shapes for example. Having them tacked to the table helps no end.

Role mats
If you are using a scheme such as reciprocal reading to support a group, utilise the mats approach by having a mat for each role. This can feature the responsibilities of each role member, so that if the children get stuck, they can refer to the mat. These don't strictly have to be A3 or A4, but are less likely to be lost if they are.

Taking it further

If you make your own mat, share it online on a platform such as Twitter and save a colleague the time of making something similar.

#workingmats

Weather forecast

'I love writing the weather forecast.'

Who knew that the weather could be so stimulating? Intervention starters involving the weather are brilliant for leading a group into a task that is relevant to the knowledge or skills you are working on.

Symbols

Have the different weather symbols – e.g. cloudy, rain, sunshine – in the intervention space, with paper underneath them. The first to arrive has to choose the symbol that best matches the weather outside. Everyone else has to write a different word for that weather format.

Temperature and rain checks

If you are near an outdoor space, get a garden thermometer and record the temperature. You can do this together on a chart or (and this will propel you into stardom) you can let the children write the temperature in YOUR teacher diary. I have never seen or met another teacher who lets the children write in their diary and it really is the ultimate reward.

Similarly, measure the rainfall in centimetres since you last measured it. Both these tasks are brilliant for real-life maths scales.

Predictions

Look at the current weather. Talk about yesterday's weather and discuss how it has changed to now. Make a prediction about how the weather will be tomorrow and write it down. This is one of the few opportunities the children will have to write genuinely about the future tense. Next time you are with the group, check back and see how accurate their predictions were.

Teaching tip

Combine all of these activities together and make it a daily display on your working weather wall.

#weatherforecast

Foam pockets

'This was the most fun phonics lesson EVER.'

This idea needs just two items, found in any supermarket, yet which last for ages. You will find them irresistible to use even as an adult!

Teaching tip

Check beforehand that no one is allergic to any of the materials.

Taking it further

Why not write letters on lighter card and hide these letters with the foam pockets? Swipe through the foam and see if the children can identify the letter from what they can see.

Bonus idea ★

Glitter in the pockets can make this extra special!

#foampockets

From shape work to letter formation, the foam pocket will help you again and again. Although using the word 'kinaesthetic' may well bring about shivers in some people, these are gloriously tactile tools.

Buy some zipper-style sandwich bags and fill them a third full with the cheapest shaving foam you can source. Slowly squeeze them shut, pushing out as much of the air as possible, then seal them up tightly. Flatten them and have some dark card handy.

Sitting the foam pockets over the card, ask the children to write a letter through the plastic. The foam should shift out of the way, revealing the dark colour underneath, and will stay pretty clear until wiped clean.

These can be used countless times in a lesson, and when they become exhausted, simply top up with more foam.